THE CASE METHOD OF INSTRUCTION

A RELATED SERIES OF ARTICLES

EDITED BY

CECIL E. FRASER

FIRST EDITION

McGRAW-HILL BOOK COMPANY, INC.

NEW YORK AND LONDON

1931

FOREWORD

THE most significant thing about the use of cases is the great elasticity that they offer the individual instructor in developing his own teaching methods. The usefulness of cases varies from their inclusion as illustrative material in a course consisting largely of lectures or textbook assignments to their use as a foundation for a course conducted entirely by discussion. The one common fact in this system of pedagogy is that regardless of the system followed the case approach provides every instructor with a concrete, practical problem which is the essential starting point whether he is conducting his course largely by lectures based on cases, entirely by discussion, or by a compromise between these two extremes. When courses are conducted entirely by lectures, however, and the material is largely illustrative, it is hardly proper to apply the name "case system."

Of major importance also is the extent to which the interest of the students is aroused by the study of concrete problems. They realize that they are dealing with actual business situations rather than with intangible theories and that the thought, method of approach, and principles applied in reaching a decision may be used in solving similar problems later in life. Although there is a somewhat widespread feeling that, where the treatment of the course is based largely upon the facts presented in cases, this method of instruction requires that each topic receive a uniform treatment, this is far from the actual situation. Even when lectures predominate in the conduct of a course the presentation that is forceful and that holds the interest of the student usually involves a variety of cases that are utilized in a number of different ways.

This volume is published at the suggestion of a number of teachers of business who wish to know more about the various approaches and methods of using cases. It is a collection of articles outlining the concepts of the case method by men who have had actual experience in its application. Although the ideas expressed are apparently diverse they are in agreement in their emphasis on the great elasticity of the medium from the pedagogical standpoint and on the high degree of student interest developed by the use of cases.

WALLACE B. DONHAM.

SOLDIERS FIELD, BOSTON, MASSACHUSETTS,
August, 1931.

CONTENTS

vii

CONTENTS

CHAPTER VI

viii

CONTENTS

CHAPTER XII

CHAPTER XIII

CHAPTER XIV

CHAPTER XV

THE CASE METHOD OF INSTRUCTION

CHAPTER I

AN INTRODUCTION TO THE USE OF CASES

by ARTHUR STONE DEWING

ANY formal educational method, whatever its practical handling may be, must rest on some recognizable foundation of educational theory. In spite of the never-ending conflict of educational methods, a conflict arising to some extent from the peculiar demands of each age and to some extent from the eternal conflict of human ideals, there appear to be two, and only two, essentially different theories of education. Of these theories individual opinions represent varying combinations and varying stresses of emphasis.

One theory assumes that education should consist of a brief survey of the important facts accumulated by man through the ages. The educated man is the

1

erudite man. Just as the biological development of the human individual is a brief recapitulation of the evolution of the species through eons of time, so the education of the individual should consist of a brief recapitulation of the objective experience of the race since time immemorial. General education is general accumulation. Special education consists, of necessity, of a more intensive and exhaustive cataloguing of the results of experience along a certain direction. Specialized education in chemistry is the mastery of the facts of chemistry brought up to the immediate present. The young chemist passes over in a few years' time the results which the workers of chemistry have accumulated through centuries of groping and specialized research. Education in business, according to this theory, should consist of a recapitulation of the results of business experience arranged, catalogued, systematized, and then presented without the lumber of discarded precedents. The business student would have thrown before him, with kaleidoscopic rapidity, the final and definite results of. what long experience has taught to be, on the whole, the best and most expedient methods of business conduct.

This method has great advantages. Above all, it is efficient; it is also economical of the time, the energy, and the patience of instructor and student. Further, this method produces brilliant results. A student trained under it seems to possess a sureness, a precision, a firmness of grasp remarkable for the relatively short time which he is compelled to spend in acquiring his knowledge. This efficiency and success can be obtained easily and cheaply without disrupting the present educational methods. The teacher need only learn second-hand the facts of his subject. When he has cast these into some kind of pedagogical order, he is possessed of the tools of his trade capable of producing a finished product after the modes of an approved technique.

The other method starts with an entirely different purpose and ends with an entirely different result. It does not assume, in the first place, that education consists of imparting a brief recapitulation of human experience; it does assume, however, that education must afford the training to enable the individual to meet in action the problems arising out of the new situations of an ever-changing environment.

Education, accordingly, would consist of acquiring facility to act in the presence of new experience. It asks not how a man may be trained to know, but how a man may be trained to act. It is concerned with precedents only so far as they lead to initiatives. It deals with the oncoming new in human experience rather than with the departing old.

Human thinking and the new in human experience are indissolubly bound together. The essential characteristic of all modes of thinking is that in the process somehow something new is introduced. Whether we examine thinking from the point of view of psychology or from the point of view of theory of knowledge, the conclusion is inevitable that where thinking occurs there is an element of newness involved and without this element of newness there is no thinking. If this is correct, then the accumulation of human experience does not necessarily involve thinking, because the accumulation of human experience is inevitably the taking of what is given rather than the creation of what is new. If we teach people to deal with the new in experience, we teach them to think. In fact, power to deal with the new and power to think are prag-

4

matically the same, even though logically the two expressions may not have the same connotation.

As an ideal of educational method teaching people to think has none of the conspicuous advantages of teaching accepted truths. As a method it is crude and clumsy in execution; it is inefficient, in that no scale of accomplishment can be established and empirically applied; it lacks the technical excellence ordinarily associated with good teaching and the finished art of the pedagogues. Nevertheless, the use of cases as the basis of teaching presumes a confidence in the second of these educational theories, and, if the fullest opportunities of case instruction are realized, the whole method becomes nothing but the practical application of the theory that the power of thinking and not the acquisition of facts is the ultimate of our educational ideals.

Progress in organizing and reducing human actions to law and order must be judged according to different standards than progress in the natural sciences. Within the precincts of the natural sciences, so-called facts are subject to empirical tests—the more complete and more universal these tests, the nearer they are presumed to approach the truth. Likewise, in the sphere of religion, tradition prescribes certain ostensibly permanent answers to the question of Pontius Pilate. But when one attempts to reach fixed and certain facts, not to say truths, underlying human actions, one is confronted with an intricate and disordered heteronomy of happenings apparently devoid of order or causal relation. The situation is at its worst—or, perhaps, most complex—stage when we attempt to discover order and scientific precision among the events of social economics.

Some fifteen or twenty years ago a president of the American Philosophical Association, in his annual address, selected a modern corporate security as the most complex fact of our contemporary human consciousness. If not the most complex, it is at least so complex that a science of finance is now very, very far distant from the ideal of certainty and predictability associated with the natural sciences. It is, at best, no further along than Thales trying to deduce order out of the movements of the heavenly bodies without any conception of celestial mechanics. Such is the predicament of the social scientist; such is the problem of the discovery of truth underlying human action. And, in his narrower field, such is the task of the teacher of finance who would lead his students to think through the variety and multiplicity of financial happenings and discover probabilities that are likely to occur at best three times out of five.

Cases should be used with the clear consciousness that the purpose of business education is not to teach truths—leaving aside for a moment a discussion of whether there are or are not such things as truths—but to teach men to think in the presence of new situations. There should not be a single problem in use which is not capable of at least two intelligent solutions and it would be surprising if any group of experienced business men could offer an unequivocal solution with unanimous accord to any one of them. They do, however, have this outstanding value. They are analogues of exactly the kind of problem that is confronting the business man at the present time. How surely he is able to think through to some intelligent solution will determine the extent of his individual success and his contribution to the economic prosperity of the country. Neither rests on a command of established precedents or on the uncritical allegiance to the experience of others.

Teaching by the case method is class discussion of possibilities, probabilities, and expedients—the possibilities of the combinations of very intricate facts, the probabilities of human reactions, and the expedients most likely to bring about the responses in others that lead to a definite end. Such discussion rests on the nice balancing of probable results; and in this balancing a teacher has little to contribute except a broader appreciation of the springs of human action than his pupils are likely to have developed and perhaps a greater knowledge of economic theory and its applications to contemporary business. This economic theory should have been wrought out of American industrial conditions and not represent merely reechoes of an economic theory based on the agricultural England of the middle nineteenth century. In any event, all a teacher can hope to do is to develop, first, an appreciation of the almost infinite complexity of modern business problems, second, the hopelessness of reaching a definite and unequivocal solution, and, third—like the Hegelian trichotomy—the solution of this dilemma by some carefully reasoned but, in the end, common-sense line of action. Knotty business problems are usually best met by the simplest and most aggressive response and the one covering the longest range of time. Impatience of results is a deadly sin of business as well as of the teaching of business.

It is interesting sometimes to reflect on the reasons that lie at the foundation of the marvelous success of America in the field of economic achievement. Like the Tyrians of old, we have erected a civilization on the successful working out of problems in connection with the mastery of our material environment; and in acquiring this mastery we have devised new methods, constructed new tools, and created for ourselves a new social order. At the basis of these achievements lies the distinctive power of the Puritan fathers, of the western pioneers, and of the modern business executives to grapple with new problems with courage and poised minds and without dependence on the guides of precedent and tradition.

Throughout the ages, man has been forced to meet the conditions of his ever-changing social environment and to resort to increasingly intricate modes of thought.

The hierarchy of complex changes which passes under the name of civilization has given to the individual at once a simpler natural environment and a more complex social environment. More and more he has gained control over natural law and more and more social law has gained control over him. This increasingly complex social environment, into which the young business man is thrown, requires resourcefulness, mental courage, confidence in the untried—in short, exactly those qualities which in the space of three centuries brought into existence a new nation and a new economic order. πάντα ῥεῖ, and the ideal of our business education ought to be to teach young men to meet the oncoming flow of things with the courageousness and resourcefulness of their forefathers.

CHAPTER II

BUSINESS TEACHING BY THE CASE SYSTEM [1]

by WALLACE B. DONHAM

SIXTY years ago when Professor Langdell introduced the use of selected reported decisions of the
courts into the Harvard Law School as the basis of
classroom instruction, his idea was not received with
the greatest confidence, nor was it immediately adopted
by other law schools. For years after the case system
was first introduced, its acceptance at other institutions
was slow and it continued to arouse active controversy.
Now very little is written about it. The orthodox
method of teaching law today is the case system. The
inadequacies of cases as reported in court decisions
which arise out of their failure to include many of
the most significant facts in the substantive field to
which the decision applies are becoming recognized
as a serious limitation to both research and instruction.

[1] Adapted from an article in the *American Economic
Review*, Vol. 12, No. 1, March, 1922.

Nevertheless, in law schools of the highest standards cases are used almost universally and successfully to give the severe intellectual training needed by the lawyer. They have largely displaced the more rapid but less thorough textbook and lecture method of approach. Where law cases are supplemented in the good schools, the material used is mainly that based on the concrete study of complex business or social situations. It is a fair generalization that to a greater extent than any other process the case system develops those powers of analysis and synthesis which are essential to the practice of law.

Early in the study of the problem it is necessary to analyze and state the case system as it has been developed in teaching law, for without such an analysis it is impossible to separate the essential element from the mass of technical material and practices which are customary in the teaching of law. Five points appear to stand out in such an analysis.

First, the case system of teaching law in its present form is made possible by centuries of reported decisions which form the heritage of the common law. Professor Langdell would not have developed his method if there had not been reported cases; or in all probability if the doctrine of *stare decisis* had never developed; or if the lawyer searching for light on his law problems customarily focussed his attention on the reactions of the treatise writer instead of on the decisions of the court. The case system of the teacher of law is dependent on the reported decisions of the courts and the extension of the method into other subject matters will depend on the creation of effective substitutes for these cases.

Second, the case system in practical operation is based upon a thorough classification of the subject matter made by the instructor. It assumes that the common law is a science developed by the courts from the precedents. Yet the law is far from being an exact science. In fact it has developed by the method of trial and error to perhaps a greater extent than economics. To the extent that a scientific basis is essential to the use of the case system, economics probably has at the present time an advantage in this respect over business. As a matter of fact, however, all these subjects—law, business, and economics—may broadly be considered sciences based in part on precedents and customs and in part on natural and economic laws. The underlying principles may in numerous instances be discovered by analysis and applied to new facts. After all, the assumption underlying the teaching of all such subjects (except historically) is that they are not haphazard but that they are capable of systematic presentation. If so, the principles may be taught by an inductive method, and in numerous instances the inductive teaching of economics is already being accomplished. The extension of this inductive method into a true case system of teaching business does not present insuperable difficulties arising out of the nature of the subject.

Third, the system is made practicable by compilations of books containing a limited number of cases chosen by the editor because in his opinion they best illustrate or help to develop the legal principles he wishes to teach. Given the raw material, such compilations may readily be made in other fields. We already possess a considerable group of such case books of business.

Fourth, the collected cases of the law customarily include (*a*) the statement of facts, (*b*) the limitation to an issue or legal problem, (c) the opinion of the court, and (d) the decision. All these elements or effective substitutes may be supplied in a business case to such extent as turns out to be desirable. It is of course impossible that business discussions of business problems should possess an authority comparable to the opinion of the court or that the decision arrived at with reference to a business problem should have weight comparable to the decisions of a court, but these limitations in practice often add to the vivacity of a classroom discussion. Indeed, experience clearly indicates that, although frequently wise, neither an opinion nor a decision is essential to the successful classroom use of a business case.

As the technique of presenting business cases develops, ways of including elements similar to the opinions of the court are constantly suggested. Models of analytical methods of attacking business problems may be employed in such a manner that they fulfill the teaching function of the opinion of the court.

Fifth, the general principles involved in a law case or cases are developed through the discussion of concrete decisions reached by the court on problems which actually occurred. This classroom discussion largely or wholly displaces the lecture as a medium for the presentation of principles. In operation the burden of the systematic development of the subject by and through such discussion rests heavily on the instructor. The development of thought under the case system is always from the concrete to the abstract, from the particular situation to the broad principle. The distinguishing characteristic which makes the case system of teaching law, in the hands of a competent instructor, an instrument of great power is the fact that it arouses the interest of the student through its realistic flavor and then makes him, under the guidance of the instructor, an active rather than a passive participant in the instruction. Under this participation he analyzes and thinks systematically on legal subjects. Experience demonstrates that this element of aggressive interest on the part of the student in practice develops from the consideration of a good business case to an extent not surpassed in the teaching of law.

The characteristics, therefore, which appear to be typical of the case system of the law are: the vast number of published decisions, the thorough classification of the subject, published case books, the elements in the typical law case, and the development of general principles from the discussion of individual cases. Of these elements all, with the exception of the reported cases themselves, exist already or may be supplied for teaching business. The problem of extending the system to teaching business becomes, therefore, the problem of securing the facts about properly classified business situations or cases and presenting them in such form that they may be used effectively as the basis for classroom discussion.

In presenting cases for classroom use a variety of methods and approaches is being worked out with no immediate effort for uniformity. A study of the several case books already published will illustrate the wide differences in approach adopted by different teachers and, within the subject matter of each case book, the varying types of material and methods of presentation. Only prolonged experience in actual teaching can tend to standardize types, and such experience may bring out the necessity for more rather than fewer kinds of problems. A few points, however, stand out. In the first place, much of interest is gained by including enough facts in a problem so that the case has the atmosphere and detail of reality. Moreover, in most fields of business, on account of the infinite complexity of detail, the student cannot in general afford time to study facts considered merely as facts. There are far too many of them. One advantage of the case system is that problems properly presented furnish an opportunity for the student to acquire a broad acquaintance with both technical and general information about diverse fields of industry, not by the study of dissociated facts but as an incident in the intellectual process of working out decisions. This easy and natural way of acquiring information is wholly consistent with the more important task of training the mind to analyze and reach decisions.

No cases are found ready-made. Although every question that involves decision by an executive is a case, nevertheless the business man has not crystallized these questions into the form of a case. The instructor or field agent must obtain facts which form the basis for and illustrate each point that it is desired to bring out. Then these facts, with the identity of the firm disguised, are worked into case form. The cases have been of three general types: (*a*) the determination of major policies, such as those that involve the business as a whole or its relations to other businesses, to the general public, or to the economic and social background of business; (*b*) the determination of internal policies, such as the policy to be followed in a single department; (*c*) the interpretation and application of policies to individual cases.

In numerous cases it is advisable to include both relevant and irrelevant material, in order that the student may obtain practice in selecting the facts that apply to the case in hand. Such training is essential. The case ordinarily should not require the student to collect new facts not included in the statement. The material or known facts in the main are stated and the study of the case involves the analysis and use of these facts. Moreover, the statement of facts must include much material which the business man assumes as a matter of course, for the student lacks this background. The importance of these points becomes increasingly evident. We are constantly made aware that greater emphasis must be placed on the presentation of facts in cases used for teaching business than in cases used for teaching law. The compiler of a law case book is interested mainly in teaching law and has in mind the legal method of thought, with its large measure of dependence on precedent and authority for the handling of new legal problems. Facts are needed but may be determined by *fiat*. They are therefore often summarized in a brief statement or disposed of by the finding of a court or jury. In teaching business, practices and precedents have no weight of authority behind them, but every fact of business which can be brought in is an asset to the student, giving him a broader foundation for executive judgment. He must, moreover, come to realize the extreme difficulty of really determining facts and of giving them proper relative weight. A case adequately stated, in the discussion of which it is possible for the student to say: "But I can't make out what the facts are. Why did this party to the negotiation say what he did?"—such a case may be most effective in teaching the art of negotiation.

Certain types of business cases are much more difficult to put into shape for teaching than others. For example, factory management cases, with their infinitely varied industrial background and with the limitations imposed by the factory building and equipment, are difficult to present in such a way that the student may visualize the facts clearly. There is much less difficulty in stating a case in marketing or in banking, because it requires no stretch of the imagination for the student to obtain a clear conception of the case from a printed page. This is the ordinary medium for stating such facts. For these reasons the descriptive material for cases in industrial management and accounting must be much more elaborate and much more carefully prepared than similar material in other subjects. Such difficulties suggest the necessity of developing outlines and descriptions of industrial processes in book form in a wide variety of fields to accompany case books. In this direction, however, enough has been accomplished to demonstrate that the difference between marketing and industrial management is one of degree only and that cases in industrial management may be stated effectively if effort enough can be put into the research behind the preparation and presentation of them.

There are certain differences between the use of

cases in teaching business and in teaching law. The business case generally differs from the law case in that it contains no statement of the actual decision reached by the business man. Moreover, the methods of approach by which decisions are reached are in most instances not included in any reasoned opinion similar to the opinion of the court, and generally business cases admit of more than one solution. Enough careful analyses should be incorporated in the cases to guide the student in method. In using such cases it is clearly undesirable to include comprehensive analyses in all or even in most instances, but recent classroom experience with business cases leads to the conclusion that an increasing use of analytical material is highly desirable. These differences caused some concern in the beginning, and in practice they clearly impose on the teacher of business a definite obligation to finish the classroom discussion of each case with a clean-cut summary of the reasons and analogies which appeal to him as most important for its solution. When this is done, the frequent complete absence of analytical guides in the cases has important advantages. Among these is the practical compulsion to independent thought by the student before the problem is taken up in class. Unquestionably both the technique of presenting cases for classroom purposes and classroom methods will develop through experience into something quite different from present practice. It is nevertheless clear that the case system, as we now know it, represents a substantial advance over our previous methods and that it is extending rapidly into nearly all business subjects.

The case system of teaching law has been criticized on the ground that, as a result of the primary emphasis on analytical training and of the slower nature of the Socratic process as compared with the textbooks and the lecture, much less ground is covered and that in fact the content of the law is unduly subordinated to this training of the mind. There is no doubt that the adoption of the case approach to teaching any subject will rapidly and inevitably change the emphasis from giving the student a content of facts to giving him control of the subject. This result in legal teaching the exponents of the system to consider one of the most desirable effects obtained. The criticism appears to have even less weight as applied to business teaching than to legal, for it is clearly impossible by any method of training to transmit to the student more than a comparatively small fraction of the facts of business. But certainly, if a business school fails to give a training which fits the student for the handling of new business facts and new relationships, it fails to justify its existence. Moreover, it is at least questionable whether the informational content of business cases may not be developed to such an extent that the student in a natural and even incidental way gains a real comprehension of more business facts and practices than he could gain by any of the ordinary methods.

Our experience at the Harvard Business School indicates the clear necessity of a comparatively slow start with much attention to methods of analyzing the concrete facts of which cases consist. The instructor is apt to forget the gap which exists between him and the beginner whose general acquaintance with business situations is inevitably slight. Instruction by the case system is slow at this stage for exactly the same reasons that the beginnings of a jigsaw picture puzzle are slow. It is only when the background develops so that relationships become evident that speed is possible. The results obtained by the case system, however, are cumulative in a different way than are the results of either textbooks or lectures, and if case material in business is studied in a variety of interrelated subjects over a period of two years the power attained by students in facing new situations and the general grasp of the subject matter may be eminently satisfactory.

CHAPTER III

THE DEVELOPMENT OF PRINCIPLES BY THE USE OF CASES

by Melvin T. Copeland

THE primary purpose of the case system of instruction in business education is to develop conclusions of general significance from an analysis of concrete situations. If each case were to be looked upon as standing by itself, without relation to other cases and without reference to its general significance, the only value of the use of cases would be training in analysis. It would imply that in business practice little can be learned from experience, that each problem must be handled practically *de novo* as it arises. Such an implication would not be in accord with the facts.

It is probable that such isolated analyses of cases would have more educational value than the dogmatic pronouncements which are so common under the lecture system, for, if a student merely analyzes cases, he must do some thinking, whereas under the ordinary lecture system the "student" is little more than a clumsy stenographer, taking down notes in longhand to be memorized for examination purposes.

Far more can be secured, however, from a properly developed case system than mere training in analysis. If the cases are properly selected, each is typical in its main point or points of other situations and in contrast with still other sets of conditions. For example, take the experience of a manufacturing company which some years ago sold preferred stock to the retailers who distributed its products. The purpose of selling stock to its customers was incidentally to secure additional capital for the company, but primarily to enlist the assistance of retailers in sales promotion. In 1921 this particular company found itself short of funds. It had suffered losses from inventory shrinkage and other causes. It needed to conserve its cash. The question was: Should it pass the dividends on the preferred stock, which was largely held by retailers?

When that case is presented with full details, the students can make an analysis and draw a conclusion. If that is as far as the case is utilized, however, emphasis is thrown on the answer as to the best means of extricating the company from an embarrassing situation. In such a case as that, the best way out is likely to be a method of expediency. But, instead of leaving the case there, suppose we ask whether any basic errors had been made by the company in devising or operating its financial plan. Through a series of questions and comparisons with other cases we may arrive finally at the conclusion that the manufacturer was unwise in the first instance in tying his sales promotion program into his financial program, because of the likelihood of such a contingency's arising as was experienced in 1921. Thus a conclusion of general significance has been reached. The same conclusion, in other words, could be applied to many other companies and would serve as a guide to them in avoiding similar embarrassment.

For teaching purposes, another case, for example one of a public utility company which had sold stock to its customers, could then be introduced effectively to present a contrasting situation. The question thus would be raised as to whether it was as disadvantageous for a public utility company to sell stock to consumers of its service as for a manufacturer to sell stock to retailers who distributed his products. The more such contrasting or seemingly contrasting situations that can be brought before the class for analysis, the greater, of course, will be the assurance with which the generalized conclusions can be stated.

The case system, properly conceived, takes the realities of life in the form of concrete experiences and from them draws conclusions of wider applicability than the solution of the problem of a single company, with recognition at the same time of the limitations on the generalizations.

If the foregoing cases were being discussed from the standpoint of finance or general business policy, other cases involving the sale of stock to employees might follow, and still other cases on the sale of stock to the executives of a company, in order to lead up to the question of the circumstances under which a company is warranted and the circumstances under which it is not warranted in making its financial policy subservient to other objectives.

The field of business management obviously is large and varied; hence the cases used must necessarily serve a variety of purposes. Some cases deal with specialized organization and operating problems of production, finance, or marketing; others with problems of control through accounting and statistical records; and still others with the problems of coordinating the various activities of a business enterprise, in order to secure a stable and effective balance. For any one of these topics different methods of approach can be used and should be used where time permits and where case material is available. If the topic is typical, furthermore—and the teacher is warranted in bringing it in only if it is typical—then eventually cases can be obtained which will illustrate the pertinent conditions and which will provide the basis for conclusions of broadening significance in the formulation of business judgments.

If the case system is to be utilized to full advantage, the cases should be selected and arranged to build up the theory of the subject inductively, step by step. Each case or group of cases should serve to bring out a particular point or series of points of general significance by means of analysis, comparison, and contrast. After the analysis of a particular case or group of cases has been concluded and specific conclusions reached on particular issues raised in the case, the questions should be asked: What is the general significance of the points brought out in this case? How broadly can the conclusions be applied to other sets of circumstances? Under what circumstances would the conclusions not hold? If certain facts in the particular case were modified, how would the conclusion be altered? When a difference in conclusions appears in two or more cases on similar subjects, it is pertinent to inquire: What are the circumstances which lead to nominally conflicting decisions? In practice, the cases furnish concrete material for specific questions suggested by the foregoing abstract query. The instructor can also draw on facts of general knowledge in numerous instances to bring out the degree to which the conclusion can be generalized.

The generalized conclusions arrived at in this way are the principles of business management. They furnish a framework of theory developed from the discussion of realistic situations and give the student an intellectual background for dealing with actual problems in business life in a manner which cannot be duplicated with equal effectiveness by any other educational method yet advanced.

By having cases selected from a variety of industries, the student can be taught to discriminate between those factors which are peculiar to a given company or a given industry and those which are common to numerous companies or industries. By using concrete problems that arise in industry, the case system is made realistic and corresponds to actual business experience. By utilizing problems from a variety of industries, tying them together, and differentiating between contrasting situations to bring out both the pertinent generalizations and the limitations thereto, the case system of instruction can be employed to provide a training which rarely can be secured except over a long period of time in actual business employment. It is the development of principles from the analyses of concrete problems, therefore, which makes the case system of instruction a powerful educational tool.

CHAPTER IV

THE USE OF CASES IN THE CLASSROOM

by CECIL E. FRASER

THE increasing use of the case system is due in a measure to its easy adaptability to almost any approach an instructor may desire. No matter what text he uses or what opinions he holds, he finds that the effectiveness of his teaching is increased when his students understand and appreciate the problems of actual business. Every instructor is constantly illustrating his point of view with concrete examples. Cases which present in essential detail the significant and interesting facts of a business situation are a natural outgrowth of this habit and form perhaps the soundest basis for both theoretical and practical instruction.

Although college students are anxious to visualize actual conditions in business, their experience is so limited that in many instances it is difficult for them to apply textbook generalizations. Instruction by the case method supplies the reality such students wish and also enlists the efforts of men who otherwise might find the subject lacking in interest by giving them a glimpse of the romance of business and by stirring their imaginations as to the future development of our economic and business life.

The value of practical experience or its equivalent is universally recognized by executives. The old-fashioned way was for each man to acquire his own business education through a long period of apprenticeship. Much of his work was drudgery, often the lessons he learned were not applicable to later events, and, in an age when suspicion and secrecy were governing motives, seldom was an opportunity given to profit by the experience of others.

While not a complete substitute for a knowledge of business gained at first hand, the use of the case system materially shortens the time which a man must spend in business life before he is equipped to hold an important position. It recasts the significant bits of experience of the past; it eliminates so far as possible the drudgery of long months of unimportant or routine work; and it concentrates attention on the strategic factors in determining industrial policies. Of necessity placing himself in the position of the business man who faced the problem, the student sees through his own eyes the difficulty to be overcome and the probable consequences of a wrong decision.

Under the old apprentice method significant events in the life. history of a business often went unnoted because no one was conscious of their importance. When, as under the case system, the study of business experience takes place under the direction of a trained instructor, the significance of events is noted and strategic points are emphasized. The real lesson of the incident set forth in the case is brought home forcibly and the study proceeds from one case to the next in organized fashion under trained leadership instead of under the erratic guidance of chance.

The great leaders of industry have been most noted for their adaptability and resourcefulness in meeting new conditions. Conversely, the great failures of industry have been men who have come to grief through their inability to meet new conditions in a changing industry where business is essentially dynamic. With the rapid developments taking place in aviation, chemistry, communication, and the other great industries, who can predict the problems of the future? It is by training the student to meet the challenge of the business questions of today rather than by giving him descriptive information alone that he will be best fitted to win the battles of tomorrow.

The satisfaction which comes to an instructor using the case system lies primarily in the fact that there is no ironclad or specified plan which he must follow. It is possible for him not only to rearrange the order of the cases or the order of the divisions under which the cases may be grouped, but it also is possible for him to use the cases in class in an infinite variety of ways. Perhaps the four most common methods may be described briefly as follows:

1. *As illustrative material:* When the inexperience or immaturity of students makes descriptive lectures and standard texts desirable, the effectiveness of the course still may be increased by illustrating each point by a real case. Problems help to crystallize ideas which the student otherwise may feel are vague and intangible.

2. *As a basis for general discussion:* When students can be led to take an active part in the discussion of

cases, not only is their interest aroused to a greater degree than when problems are used as illustrative material, but the effectiveness of the instruction is increased through the actual development of the proper solution to a problem by the student rather than by the instructor. After the person conducting the course has started the discussion by asking a question intended to arouse a difference of opinion, the students then may be allowed to continue the discussion, either as they volunteer or as the instructor calls upon them.

3. *As a basis for specific questions and answers:* To avoid the loss of time which may occur in the use of the more general discussion method and to direct the class work along more definite lines, a professor may desire to follow the practice of asking a specific question of each student and requiring a complete and definite answer in return. This practice encourages calling on every man in the class in turn and facilitates obtaining an exact grade on the daily work. It forces the student to make a more careful analysis than he might otherwise and to reach a soundly reasoned conclusion.

4. *As a basis for detailed cross-examination:* In

order to simulate an actual executive conference, the person in charge of the course may prefer to follow an even more aggressive method. Under this plan the instructor prepares in advance a detailed list of questions; each initial question should have, so far as practicable, only two possible answers. For each of these answers the instructor prepares an additional question to force the student to substantiate, in detail, the position he has taken. When the discussion of the individual points of the problem has been completed, other members of the class may be asked to summarize the main factors to be considered in reaching a decision, to state the decision that should be made, and to substantiate this decision with sound reasoning. Still others may be asked to point out the principles or precedents which may apply to other problems.

From actual experience, it appears that the fourth method is the most desirable. It not only forces the student to make a thorough and practical analysis and to substantiate both the method and results of that analysis under cross-examination, but to separate from a large amount of detail the important principles on which the theory of business must be developed. As a rule, students trained in the last method have shown themselves to be better fitted to meet the problems of business than those whose preparation has been of a less rigid nature. The first three methods, however, should be used from time to time to give variety, to enable the instructor to cover ground more rapidly on some of the less important phases, and to maintain interest.

Occasionally the transition from a lecture and text-book form of teaching to the use of the case system gives an instructor a feeling of uncertainty. Many a professor, not entirely satisfied with his first attempt to use the case system in place of a series of smoothly flowing lectures, has been surprised to find that his students have not shared his uneasiness. Perhaps the most conclusive evidence of the value of the case system comes from graduates who feel that it has materially shortened their period of probation and made it possible for them to take advantage of opportunities leading to more rapid advancement.

CHAPTER V

THE CASE METHOD OF TEACHING MARKETING

by NEIL H. BORDEN

MARKETING is a field as yet little developed. The facts and guiding principles to be taught are not well defined or classified. It accomplishes little in teaching the subject merely to give a description of marketing processes, for marketing methods are in a state of rapid flux. Moreover, description does not lead the student into a consideration of the basic problems of the field, nor is it likely to stimulate active thinking about them. It is true that in recent years more and more valuable treatises on various aspects of marketing and textbooks dealing comprehensively with the various phases of the subject as far as it has been developed have appeared and, if properly used, offer satisfactory teaching media. Yet there remains the indisputable fact that it is essential for both the teacher and the student to form the habit, not merely of thinking correctly about individual marketing problems, but of attempting as well to develop relationships between phenomena as a means of securing precedents to apply in further analysis. For a field in which we know so little, relatively, such habits of thought are especially to be desired, and in securing them the case method presents exceptional opportunities for both student and teacher.

To the marketing teacher an extensive collection of cases offers an opportunity to learn and think about marketing problems as they actually occur in business. Through analysis and comparison of cases, an opportunity both to classify basic information concerning the field and to determine precedents and guiding principles is offered. The larger the number of cases available on common or similar problems the more likely are sound precedents concerning such problems to be derived. It is the experience of the instructors in marketing that a continuing study of cases has resulted in constant reclassification of knowledge about the subject and the determination of an increasing number of significant precedents. The case method is an excellent one by which to pioneer in an undeveloped field of study. It furnishes the material, often unavailable otherwise, from which to reason.

The case system gives a sense of reality to both student and teacher which heightens interest. The cases not only appear real, but they are actual reports of business situations. Working with actual information, both teacher and student are able to avoid the dangers of arm-chair reasoning. Through a wide study of cases, they acquire what is equivalent to a background of actual business experience. Cases, moreover, supplement such practical experience as teacher and student may have and thus broaden their horizons.

It is highly essential for the man going into active work in marketing to be alert both in crystallizing the problems which may come before him and also in thinking these problems through. The case method, properly used, should accomplish these objectives. It fosters the habit of thinking in terms of problems or issues. A problem or issue once crystallized is well on its way to solution. The student becomes cognizant of the importance of ferreting out the facts that may apply to any situation. He develops constructive imagination in trying to find solutions to perplexing situations; and in marketing the employment of constructive imagination is highly essential to success.

If he has been properly trained in case use, the marketing student turned executive will have the teacher's habit of attempting to lay down sound precedent from his experiences. He will seek to relate any problem with which he deals to others with which he has dealt or which he has studied. Thereby he will seek broader significances than may appear at first in any current problem; moreover, significant precedents already derived will help him to arrive at sound conclusions.

The case method, then, develops valuable habits of thought for the man going into the marketing field. It has high possibilities for inculcating in a student the ideal of self-education, the only true education.

Marketing instruction should not only give the student training in proper thinking about his subject, but it should also give him a background of factual material and a knowledge of sources of information which will serve as tools in his thinking processes. The case method can accomplish this objective also.

At times the case method as applied to business has been criticized on the ground that students do not have the background of factual material with which to do their thinking. This criticism is not basic, for it is always possible to build into cases the factual material essential for their analysis. It is possible, also, to indicate sources of information which may be required outside of the case. Marketing, moreover, adapts itself more fortunately than some business subjects to case presentation, even for students without any previous business experience, for almost every student has had opportunity to observe marketing methods and has had numerous occasions for dealing with marketing agencies. Accordingly, he has a background into which case presentation may well fit. From his own background of observation, from the factual material written into cases, and from source material indicated, the student may build gradually a broad, factual knowledge of the field of marketing and learn of sources of data open to him.

CHAPTER VI

THE CASE METHOD OF TEACHING BUSINESS
STATISTICS

by JOSEPH L. SNIDER

SINCE the use of statistics is one of the outstanding characteristics of modern business administration, there is perhaps a natural tendency for students of this subject to attach greater importance than is deserved to the statistical approach. It seems wise, therefore, to recognize the limits beyond which the statistical approach cannot be effective. There are so many aspects of a business problem which cannot be measured statistically that the field in which "business judgment," without statistical support, must be relied upon remains very large.

Nevertheless, there is a great variety of problems in the solution of which statistics are useful. These problems may be grouped in two classes which are not mutually exclusive but are sufficiently distinct to warrant separation. A business organization is affected very greatly by the changing conditions in the industry of which it is a member and by the fluctuations of business in general. There are thus numerous problems which, in their origin, are essentially external to the individual organization. Many other problems have their origin within the individual business concern. Statistics may play a very useful part in handling problems in both these broad classes.

The study of statistics relating to the conditions of particular industries and to general business conditions is well adapted to the case method of instruction. A type of introductory problem that is particularly effective is one that involves forecasting the price of a commodity. This offers perhaps a natural transition from the study of elementary economic principles to the consideration of business problems. An estimate of the probable future price of a commodity is, of course, of considerable value to the business concerns which handle the commodity in question and is the sort of problem set primarily by conditions outside the individual business. Several actual commodity price forecasts may be considered involving not only the forecast and the measure of its success or failure but also the data and reasoning through which the forecast was made.

In a study of the conditions in a particular industry the sampling process is necessary. Three or four of the leading industries of the country may be selected. Questions which may constantly be asked in this section of the course are:

1. What statistical data are currently available in this industry?

2. Where may the data be obtained?

3. What do the data indicate as to the present condition and the outlook in this industry?

A study of general business conditions also requires a certain amount of sampling. The study should cover the most important current measures in the various divisions of business in the aggregate such as the activity of industry and trade, commodity prices in general, the security markets, and the money markets.

A consideration of the *measures* of general business fluctuations leads to a consideration of the problem of general business forecasting. This involves a reference to the most valuable methods of forecasting and an estimate of the possibilities and limitations in handling this problem.

One does not have to proceed very far in the use of statistics in connection with business problems to realize that the figures used require analysis. The term "analysis" embraces a considerable number of statistical methods such as time series analysis and the construction of index numbers. Accurate interpretation of the current record of business activity, for example, requires the measurement of seasonal variation and long-time growth. Further, changes in the general price situation cannot be measured without the construction of some sort of aggregate, which involves the problem of index-number construction. Attention to methods of construction and interpretation of various types of graph is also important. These and other statistical methods can probably be handled in most effective fashion through the means of laboratory hours where the technique of statistical method is applied to a particular problem. The purpose of a study of statistical methods is not to train technical statisticians but to develop an understanding of the most important statistical "tools," sufficient to enable one to use them in making interpretations of current data. Case material has been found especially helpful in the laboratory instruction. Cases show concretely the place and importance of statistical methods in studying business problems.

Problems which in their origin are peculiarly internal to a business organization are of substantial importance. A natural transition from external to internal problems results from the study of the effects upon different types of business concerns of changes in general business; for example, it is important to know how a manufacturer of raw material is likely to be affected in contrast to a retail distributor. It is important also to know how a manufacturer or retailer compares with other firms in his field as to volume of sales, expenses, and percentage of net profit. Then, too, the broad topic of market analysis lends itself to statistical treatment. An understanding of the probable market for the product of a particular company as distinguished from the probable market for another type of product and company often means the difference between success and failure.

Problems which are more particularly internal are

concerned with the statistical analysis of sales, the break-down of aggregate sales by type and their distribution as to locality. Another problem of considerable importance relates to the analysis of inventories, particularly with relation to sales.

A further consideration of internal business problems involves the use of statistics in the setting of standards of performance with reference to certain aspects of the business such as production efficiency, sales effort, labor turnover, machine utilization, and collections of accounts receivable. These topics are, of course, only illustrative since the possibilities of selection are wide and are chiefly limited by the availability of suitable case material. The general aim of the instruction is to make clear the usefulness and limitations of statistical measurements in handling business problems. The purpose is not to develop trained statisticians but to make one somewhat better prepared (when later one is engaged in nonstatistical work) to use intelligently the results of statistical work done by others.

Although the preceding discussion relates to introductory work, much of it applies also to more advanced work in statistical analysis in which the statistical methods are considered largely from the viewpoint of the business executive rather than the technical statistician. A special research course gives opportunity for those who wish to focus their attention upon technical matters, while a course dealing particularly with business conditions takes up problems of this type in greater detail than can be done in a general course.

Reference has already been made to certain subjects which lend themselves particularly to treatment by the case method. This method has in fact been found effective for most of the work in a general course. In addition to cases in the strict sense, that is, a record of actual experience by an individual business concern, certain other material, which may be included under a broader definition of case material, has been found valuable. By this is meant, for example, the discussion in a leading trade journal of the position and outlook of a given commodity or an article in a financial journal dealing with some problem of significance to the business community as a whole. In addition to case material in this broader sense, occasional lectures and a small amount of textbook material seem to have a place. These other methods of instruction are employed partly because they seem better adapted for certain subjects, partly because case collecting has not yet covered all the topics that might well be covered, and also partly because variety in methods of instruction seems to be effective.

CHAPTER VII

THE CASE METHOD OF TEACHING FINANCE

by GEORGE E. BATES

FINANCE suffers, perhaps, from being, like accounting, one of the older business subjects in which formal
instruction has been given. In the standardization of
definition and concepts which develops in the course of
time there lurks the dangers of an unimaginative and
prescriptive pedantry. Timeworn trails are useful, but
they often discourage exploration and the choice of
routes better suited to the ever-changing demands of
a progressively more dynamic society.

An outstanding contribution of the case method to
the subject of finance has been its implicit requirement of reappraising accustomed paths. A traditional
approach to the teaching of money and banking, for
example, is historical in the genetic sense. Class after
class has proceeded up the trail from barter to current financial organization and with each class it has

become more difficult, as the trail has lengthened, to place the student in an unbiased position to evaluate the contemporary banking organism in all its true, current implications. Instructors aware of this pedagogical difficulty have reversed the educational process and with their classes have first examined the existing financial structure, freeing their students from traditional bias and encouraging an imaginative approach too often lacking in the former method. Case instruction has been an invaluable tool in assisting and encouraging this rearrangement, not so much of materials as of viewpoint. In skillful hands it has proved of incalculable value in stimulating a free play of imagination and in engendering that zest for the subject which insures an acquisition of so much of the historical and contemporary background as may be found useful in appraisal or explanation.

The teacher of finance is first confronted with the choice between material or precept and power. As stated elsewhere in this book, the balance seems to rest with power, though power without material would be as abstract in finance as in mechanics. The use of cases, although undertaken for developing the necessary power of recognition, analysis, and solution of financial problems, nevertheless adequately provides the essential material in a far more romantic guise than is possible under a preceptive system. Such material is current, concrete, and is developed only in the most natural manner, through application.

If the finance teacher have uppermost in mind the presentation of the spirit and point of view of his subject, training in the induction of generalizations, and the development of power to cope with new problems possibly involving new sets or patterns of materials, rather than a survey and fixation of past factual material, then the problem of defining his field is less acute. He will employ the sampling method, selecting cases designed to give the desired training without undue concern for encroachment upon other subjects in the business curriculum. Indeed, finance, outside the highly specialized sense of the marketplace for certain financial media, scarcely exists apart from an extremely close correlation with the functions of production and distribution. The remarkable merit of the case system here is that it constantly forces upon the consciousness of student and instructor this fundamental correlation and precludes the idea, too often prevalent under the lecture system, of an air-tight compartment of finance, a conception induced in the first instance by the artificial division of business administration into teaching units.

The manner in which finance shall be approached for teaching purposes depends upon the general pattern of the curriculum. If two or more years be assumed for the business curriculum, an introductory course in finance would probably parallel such major-division courses as production and distribution and such auxiliary courses as accounting and possibly statistics, while general economics would be assumed as prerequisite to matriculation or a course in business economics would be offered at least in the first half-year. It is in this introductory year's work that the case system offers an opportunity for correlation and economy of effort that has as yet been little capitalized. Reference is made to the possibility of developing cases which may be used in more than one of the basic courses. The financial aspects of such cases might be discussed in the finance course and the marketing, manufacturing, accounting, and statistical aspects in those other courses. It would probably be impossible to extend this method to more than a portion of the year's work, because of the differences in approach and emphasis and the inherent limitations of the cases, but it does open an exceedingly desirable field for experimentation.

It is not unlikely that the use of the case method in the introductory course will work a gradual change in outlook and content. Any change, in fact, would be gradual because of the multiplied precedents for teaching such a course. An introductory course has so long been looked upon as a survey course that its real purpose of forming an introduction to the subject may be lost in the inevitable extension of the survey, till all that remains is a superficial smattering, a vocabulary, and a false sense of knowledge, no firm grasp or power. With the widening horizons of the introductory course today, it may be found advisable to examine more thoroughly a lesser number of cases at the sacrifice of some material coverage. The disadvantages of the general survey course would not be so great if all students followed it with the more intensive training of advanced courses, but this is frequently precluded for those specializing in other fields of business. If a fairly complete survey of the material content of the subject were contemplated, the lecture and text method, with the use of cases merely as illustrative matter, would seem to be indicated as more economical of time. If power is the goal, however, it seems that experience would dictate the use of selected cases, in number no greater than could be adequately grasped within the given time.

Advanced instruction in finance is frequently divided among four courses: corporation finance, commercial banking, investment banking, and investments, to represent, respectively, the points of view of the corporation, the short-term creditor, the middleman for longer-term credits and capital, and the capitalist. In view of the inter-relations of commercial and investment banking, these courses are sometimes combined; and a course on investments or investing is occasionally omitted in the belief that it might be substantially little more than another correlation course, in instances where an advanced correlation course in business policy is offered, and that the cases used in many other, and especially the other finance, courses do provide fairly satisfactory training from the standpoint of the investor. The finance peculiar to certain industries will also usually be touched upon in such specialized courses as real estate or public utility management, while a correlation course in business policy would inevitably include many problems of financial aspect.

It is in the advanced courses that the case method has been found indispensable, partly because current raw material for portions of the courses is available only in the cases and partly because the case discussion method has been found the most effective for this more intensive training in power.

An important distinction has been evolved between the handling of cases in the introductory and in the advanced finance courses. For the former, there has been a tendency to select a simplified type of case with a clear issue or problem stated and with much of the obscuring garnishment of the actual situation stripped away. This procedure gives beginning students a familiarity with the field and a training in the analysis of stated problems. In the more advanced work, experiment has been made with cases in which no issue is stated, editorially, and the greater amount of the involved setting of the actual business situation included. The extension of this method will mean longer cases, slower progress with material content, and smaller classes, but it may overcome a noticeable inability of students, however well trained in resolving the stated problem, to recognize and define fundamental issues in business situations shrouded in all the complexities of actuality. Despite the obvious disadvantage that this procedure is as much slower than the problem method as that method is than the lecture system, its value will be realized when it is remembered that it is the unrecognized, unstated problem in business which usually proves most costly. The problem perceived and defined is well on its way toward solution, or, if readily apparent, it is highly probable that it existed in an embryonic and curable stage for a long period and only forged into prominence when anything short of a drastic and expensive remedy would have been futile.

To encourage experimentation in the case method, it is still desirable that practically no restrictions be placed upon the types of cases reported or the manner of their classroom presentation. An examination of the finance cases in current use discloses a great many variations, though for the most part they may be classified under the general headings of problem cases and case histories. The former are simplified cases in which the editor has supplied a clear statement of the issue or appended questions involving the issue. In the case history there is less editorial focusing of the issue and, if given, the statement of problems involved is that of the corporation, firm, or individual furnishing the case material. This type of case may be written around a particular problem or a complex situation involving a number of issues. When specific problems are recognized in these cases, such solutions as were actually considered or tried are usually presented. There are also occasional cases of historical import with primary emphasis on material, technique, or procedure, and these are most frequently employed as introductions to other cases where the problems may be thrown into greater relief through the contrast thus afforded.

In the use of cases for teaching finance there are almost as many variations as there are individual instructors. This, in itself, is a happy commentary on the case method. Observation over a considerable period would indicate, in general, a half dozen steps in the normal progress toward an exclusive use of cases in the classroom, the development being somewhat as follows: cases being used (1) as illustrative material to parallel the lecture method, (2) as preparatory background for lectures, (3) as points of departure for discussion of the major problems in a field, (4) to supplement the text with materials and problems too recent for adequate textbook coverage, (5) in combination with lectures and text, each particular medium being employed at its seemingly most effective stages in the course, and (6) as the basis for a progressive discussion to cover an outline of material, where the problems may be considered as the material.

Once the finance course is entirely upon a case basis, the technique may be varied by employing selected cases to emphasize the point of view, the recognition of problems, and the analysis aimed at solutions, without necessarily covering a complete outline of content, or, when time permits and the case material is adequate, arranging in each minor division of the course for preliminary study of leading cases typical of extremes, followed by discussion of border-line cases which fix the rule or generalization.

The extreme flexibility of the case method affords the instructor almost unlimited freedom in the choice of his materials and the adaptation of method to his particular views and requirements and allows him as ample a definition of his subject and as generous correlation with other subjects as his enthusiasm and the necessities of the general business curriculum may dictate.

CHAPTER VIII

THE CASE METHOD OF TEACHING ACCOUNTING

by THOMAS H. SANDERS AND ROSS G. WALKER

ACCOUNTING was one of the earliest phases of business to be systematized and appropriated for college-course purposes. For this reason it is often regarded as having arrived at a greater degree of maturity and definition, as an educational subject, than such fields as, say, marketing or industrial management; the aims, scope, and materials of accounting are supposed to be better organized and more generally agreed upon. In so far as this impression is true, it may be doubted whether, and how far, the alleged state of accounting is an advantage. If a subject becomes crystallized too early, or in an era when educational philosophy is less intelligent or less comprehensive than might be wished, it becomes liable not only to the charge of being insufficient; it takes on a formal rigidity which is an indication that its inherent quality has been missed, that its vitality has gone. Something of this sort, it is to be feared, had occurred in accounting; at least it was widely charged, especially by critics not directly engaged in the teaching of accounting, that the treatment of the subject had become entirely too mechanistic.

The more progressive of accounting instructors heeded this criticism; in fact they have themselves been among the foremost of the critics. Within recent years attempts have been made, in several directions, to make instruction in accounting a more effective instrument for the social and business purposes it is intended to serve. First, there has been a widespread revision of the pedagogical processes by which the subject has been imparted to students; ideas such as the "balance-sheet approach," the "income approach," all represent a reaching after the vital elements in the subject. Second, books have been written [1] which have omitted all reference to bookkeeping or the compilation of records, concentrating rather on definition and interpretation of balance sheet and income statement. A third class

[1] HATFIELD, E. G., *Accounting,* D. Appleton & Company.

of literature [1] has sought to tie in accounting concepts more closely with economic concepts, and to explain why at certain points accounting practice has seen fit to diverge from economic theory. Fourth, the attempt has been made to treat accounting as an instrument for the solution of certain problems of the business man and to consider the instrument directly from that point of view. What, it is asked, are the problems of the business man? To which of these may accounting make a contribution? What contribution does the business man expect from accounting? How may accounting most effectively render this service? These are the basic questions in the mind of an instructor who essays to deal with accounting by the case method. All teachers who have had experience in the matter, and business men who have employed men of various training, will unite in agreeing upon the wide disparity in the results obtained by approaching what is ostensibly the same body of material from opposite points of view.

It immediately becomes apparent that those in-

[1] CANNING, J. B., *The Economics of Accountancy,* The Ronald Press Company.

terested in accounting are not a single group, and their expectations from accounting are likewise varied; their questions cannot all be dealt with alike, nor answered by the same figures and statements. It next develops that accounting is far from being an exact science; its statements are not composed of unquestioned facts nor of immutable figures—they are largely matters of opinion, estimates of future events and contingencies. One of the highest accounting authorities in the United States said that a balance sheet is nothing more than a guess, though, he added, the guess of the experienced man will carry far greater weight than that of the novice. No rules of thumb can wholly avail here; questions of reasonable judgment come up in a way analogous to the application of the rule of reason in law. Where quantities are not demonstrable with mathematical precision, what would be the judgment of the reasonable man, possessed of adequate information and intelligence?

Sometimes the reasonable and intelligent men cannot be the criterion for the accounting presentation; if many of those interested are neither reasonable nor intelligent, their probable reactions must nevertheless be anticipated and considered. To take an extreme case, suppose a bank has, for any reason one cares to assume, become temporarily embarrassed by having some of its liquid assets become frozen for the time being; suppose that all who really know the facts believe that the situation involves no real danger, but that the difficulties will be satisfactorily cleared up before any damage is done. But suppose that, if this temporary situation were published in a statement, with all the difficulties literally expressed, it might lead to alarm among depositors and encourage a run on the bank. What should be shown in its statement at this time? Should it be, in substance, its inherently sound condition, the condition which all those with information believe to be the actual condition for all practical and permanent purposes, or should it be the temporarily embarrassed position which the literal-minded man might wish to call the "present condition of the business"? Or to take another situation of more general application: When in 1920 and 1921 the decline in security prices was so drastic, at what values should they be shown in the balance sheets of insurance and other companies whose assets were mostly in securities? Should they be shown at current market and thus indicate an alarming deficiency of assets?—or should it be said, as was the fact, that there was neither need nor intention of realizing on these securities at present prices, that the securities were held for the purpose of meeting the company's obligations over a long period of time, and that they would without doubt suffice to do so? These are but typical of a thousand questions which cannot be answered from textbook prescriptions but require the application of a reasonable judgment to the circumstances of the individual case. It is in the making of such analyses, and the use of such judgment, that the case method is designed to provide early exercise.

It is not enough to say that the purpose of the classroom is to teach a man to think, as the current expression goes. In regard to thinking, its purpose is to train in *accuracy* of thinking, to teach the art of making seasoned judgments and of giving those judgments concrete expression in carrying on the business of life. But the purpose of the classroom extends still further. We should not forget that among the purposes of the class hour are training in the philosophy of the subject studied, as distinguished from the mechanics of its practical utilization, and in that knowledge of the world which any study faithfully pursued can give us. In regard to this last, it is only necessary that our conception of the study be big enough to insure that this important by-product will be forthcoming.

On the side of the classroom, and making for its success in attaining these objectives, are the atmosphere of curiosity and debate, and the guidance of a mature student in the field covered. Ranged against it, and making for failure, are its remoteness from reality and the inevitable restraints of a formal atmosphere.

Thus, whether the emphasis is on "power" or "information," or the philosophy of that information, or some mechanistic end, good instruction will always seek to determine the probable weight of each favorable and unfavorable factor in a particular course of study, and to find means of enhancing the possible helpfulness of the good and of nullifying the harmful potentialities of the bad.

To many thoughtful students of pedagogy in accounting, the use of the preparatory text alone has run quite counter to this principle of sound instructional procedure. It seems to have assumed that, however good or bad the exposition involved, all that was ever needed was to get the statement of the theory between the covers of a book. Even where the text does not supply all the thinking, it still falls short of what can be done to make the study real. It still fails to bring about the necessary union of the subject studied with some definite purpose in life, and to supply all those varied elements of fact and of setting which are indispensable to the study of the subject as an art.

Practice in seasoned thinking in a field like accounting is altogether out of the question where the student is not only led by the hand but his judgments are confined solely to manufactured issues of a quite academic range and definition.

There is something in the atmosphere of reality, at least in the atmosphere of the research laboratory, which is indispensable to intellectual accomplishment. But in this there is nothing to discourage a teacher in the classroom; it should always be honestly admitted, and its implications of difficulty set up avowedly as the great problems of formal education. It does not mean that speculation is less important than it is supposed to be, as an educational device, or that the use of abstractions in the development of principle is any less valuable than it has always been to the aggressive teacher. The proposition only serves to indicate the need for uniting the mind of the student with its concrete objectives or rather with the concrete things which are going to make up the visible world of the student's later activity.

Possibly more than anything else "a strict text diet" fails to develop the *problem* of a given field of study. This may be chargeable to the peculiar genus of the current text, but the belief is arguable that the failure is rooted in the method itself. There is no learning to hurdle without hurdling; there is no substitute in thinking, or in learning what thought is to be about, without sensing the concrete outlines of the obstacle as it has become a part of life, and as it gave birth to the study of which it constitutes the subject matter.

It has been said that true education comes only through self-cultivation and experience. If we say that the final increment of true education comes only through self-cultivation and experience, we have probably spoken more truly. But it is this final increment which constitutes so vital a part in the sum total of an educated man's equipment. It is the pinch of seasoning which seasons the whole dish. It is that which makes education assimilable to the practical affairs of life.

Actual cases and problems based on actual cases as they have been drawn from the settings of experience meet all the tests of classroom fitness. Being real and constituting the problems of real people, they aid in making the class hour less formal, they help the student to see the principles of the study in actual affairs, they stimulate independence of thought and supply most of those *nuances* of fact and opinion which distinguish the problem of reality from the typical *example* of the schoolroom.

The study of cases and problems is a sound substitute for an intelligently guided apprenticeship, but it goes much beyond that. The study of cases in accounting, for example, not only stimulates the making of independent judgments, the balancing of the elements of seasoned opinions, but necessarily lays before the student an attractive cross-section of industry. As one moves from one case to another, one passes through many different business settings and perforce acquires that breadth of view, that varied background, which are so essential to real cultivation in the field. None of this of course precludes the supplemental use of the contributions of others in the way of speculative treatment of the issues involved. But it is probably true that this recourse to the opinions of others should follow upon a rigorous first experience with actual problems rather than precede such an experience and thus greatly weaken the likelihood that the student will develop self-reliance.

The solution of the typical formal problem in accounting is largely an arithmetical matter, with some latitude here and there for interpretation. But in actual business the determination of what the problem is, what the business setting is, and what information will contribute to its solution are the first and greatest problems. It is the intention of the case method that the student, from an elementary statement of the bare facts of the situation, should first define for himself the nature of the accounting problem and then reason out the approach to a solution, instead of being given in advance a formula to lean on.

The experience of students when first confronted with cases of this sort is interesting to observe. Their earliest reaction is one of bewilderment. "We have no facts to go upon" is their complaint, meaning that, as in most instances of actual life, the facts are incomplete, or insufficient to point unmistakably to a conclusion. "What is the answer?" is their next query, as they revert to the textbook attitude of mind and wish to be told immediately the rule or method of solution. As they proceed with more and more cases, still finding no answers in the incomplete statements, no rules for their guidance, they are apt to flounder more and develop a spirit even of resentment and annoyance, which is simply the measure of their natural antipathy to doing that most difficult of all things—their own thinking.

Reference has been made to balance-sheet problems; similar examples might be drawn from the income statement. Here again the man of experience knows that any income statement is largely contingent and provisional. Not only must a valuation be placed upon inventories of materials and merchandise, but the disposition of large amounts of expenditure must be determined before a net-income figure is obtained. For the practical business man the income statement is not a matter of mere passive or academic interest; it is likely to become a basis of early action. What profits are available for distribution to owners, for expansion of the plant, for undertaking advertising or marketing campaigns? What profits are available to secure the repayment of bankers' loans or other obligations? What profits may be shown which would serve as a basis for purchase or sale of the entire business? It is sometimes asserted that the facts are the facts, regardless of the uses to which they are to be put. The assertion has an element of truth in it but is too often made the occasion for a perfunctory performance of accounting work, when what is needed is a clear comprehension of the purposes which the statement must serve and the explicit presentation of information which will answer those purposes.

This does not mean the warping of facts to serve a particular end. Accounting has been the subject of two contrary lines of criticism. While some people have scored accountants because their statements were not instruments of business policy, others have scored them because they were. These groups represent the conflicting interests in business bargains. A group of men preparing a business for sale will naturally dress it up to look its best in the balance sheet and operating statements; in this process they are tempted to become irritated with the accountant who desires that they keep themselves within what he regards as the limits of the facts; they want to use the statements as instruments to serve a specific policy.

CHAPTER IX

THE CASE METHOD OF TEACHING INDUSTRIAL MANAGEMENT

by JOHN GURNEY CALLAN

EXPERIENCE in manufacturing, as in other business fields, presents itself naturally through dealings with a moving and changing group of interdependent situations, each calling for action or decision to be determined from all direct or related requirements in the light of relevant experience and analogies; in this fundamental respect case methods in teaching simulate the approach to which men interested in manufacturing problems must become adapted and accustomed.

In studying manufacturing cases, as in dealing with other business problems, it is important that no facts having possible bearing be left out of soundly estimated account; business cases are like those in medicine or engineering rather than those in law, where facts not in the record are not in the case. Indeed, the same inevitability with which disregarded or unknown natural laws eventually obtrude themselves upon the manufacturer and upset partial solutions besets cases quite as it does practice. However, the necessary circumscription of most manufacturing cases becomes less disturbing when one remembers that the pressures of overhead costs, competition, and changing markets often make a timely though temporary working solution based upon available data even more necessary than a complete and permanent one.

A case approach to problems of production develops an embarrassing latitude as to choice and arrangement of subject matter and also some rather exacting specific requirements. A major part of the limited space here available will be given to the discussion of scope and content, and of appropriate case material, but this is not to be interpreted as a transfer of emphasis from such general benefits to be derived from case presentation as have already been discussed in the introductory chapter.

Definition of the field of industrial management

presents more than the usual difficulties. The dean of a midwestern collegiate business school has said that a tour of such schools last year disclosed fair concordance in other fundamental courses, but as many different courses in industrial management as there were schools. The name is taken here as defining an area comparable to that of the other basic courses. Some early writers and a few later ones give it a broader meaning, approximating the general management of industry and including not only production and cost accounting but some marketing and industrial finance. This inclusive conception is not discussed, but, keeping to the production of economic goods mainly in factories, there are still many sources of such diversity of approach.

The course may be shaped to the needs of classes largely preparing for work other than manufacturing, or it may be intended to fit men to make their beginning in factory production, or to broaden the executive conceptions of engineering students, as were the earliest management courses, upon which some of the later ones were founded. The subject lends itself to broad or even conventionalized treatment, with the factory rather taken for granted, and the discussion emphasizing environmental and economic factors, conditioning or determining manufacturing of various broadly defined types, and relating these to demand and to financing; or equally it lends itself to specific treatment of factory operation with accompanying necessary recognition of the existence and effect of these conditioning factors. In either case, diversified typical industries may be studied first, and generalized conclusions may afterward be built up from this industrial approach; or the reverse order may be adopted, and the functions and elements common to all manufacturing may be identified and studied first, and their adaptation to specific industries be discussed afterward. Perhaps it should not be surprising that the content of courses under this common name ranges from production economics to factory housekeeping. Discussion of the use of cases in this field will, for convenience, be centered around three different types of course, to show the general utility of the method.

A course treating the subject essentially as one in production economics may touch briefly upon production of goods elsewhere than in factories, and upon production of economic services. Factory production is considered with relatively slight attempt to ascertain just what a factory is like or exactly what goes on in it; rather it is taken as a recognized means, that plenty of operating men understand, for supplying goods of various manufacturing and selling characteristics, to meet demands having related characteristics, subject to the existing economic and physical-technical conditions and social usages and standards. Such an approach may be compared with the study of marine shipping operations without minutely detailed concern with ships or the navigation and running of them, or of public utilities with only minimum interest in generating and power-using equipment or transmission networks. There is no lack of valuable and interesting case material for such a course. It deals with concepts and terminology familiar to men who have studied elementary economics, it correlates well with other business courses, and it minimizes the difficulties with unfamiliar factory background that are spoken of later.

By way of a few illustrations of appropriate case material: Consumer demand may be studied in diverse industries, and the case discussion may develop its varying effect on manufacturing where it is primary or derived, seasonal or steady, predictable or erratic for identified reasons, and where such demand comes to the producer immediately from the consumer or where sales pass through a distribution chain carrying stocks. The character of the goods may be shown to have important reactions on the equipment, organization, and management of the manufacturing plants in which they can best be made, and on responses to conditions of fluctuating prosperity; and products may be recognized in this aspect as determinants of production. They may be producers' goods of kinds responding variously to secular trends and cyclic, seasonal, or erratic fluctuations; or they may be consumers' goods—necessities or luxuries, staples, style goods, perishables, products requiring high technical skill, sensitive to price or to quality, in relatively static or in advancing arts, adapted by their nature and the demand to be made by mass production methods or to special order. The sale may imply service, entailing provision for rendering it, or it may be final. The relation of product and equipment policy to alternative ways of financing may be developed. The financing of intermediate or ultimate buyers may be of concern as a stimulant to demand that nevertheless •shifts the time axis with contingent effect on stability of production.

Cases dealing with the factory itself in a course of this type may couch internal problems in generalized terms familiar to the economist: Tools of production for specified product and demand may be adapted to general or to increasingly special or even to single-purpose use, and this phase of equipment policy may be discussed without detailed visualization of the tools; the housing, grouping, and arrangement of these tools to fit the needs of defined and illustrated general types of "processing" on grouped types of goods may be discussed without entering very deeply into factory design. Cases without difficult factory background may deal with such subject matter as arises from various phases of division of labor and specialization as between regions, plants, and individuals, and with correlation of the subdivided effort by identified types of management, planning, and supervision. Similar treatment is suitable for transfer of skill and of thought; factors determining diminishing or increasing returns from the factory as a whole, from items of equipment, and from personnel; relation of inventory fluctuation to stabilization of employment, subject to character of product and demand and to working-capital policy; least-cost combinations responsive to changes in single and grouped variables. In such a course the cases dealing with employment relations may well be approached from the viewpoint of the sociologist and the psychologist, as well as from that of the factory personnel man.

A course of different and more usual type gives some prefatory background material and then moves its point of view into the factory and takes up in sequence the grouped internal divisions and components, and the executive and operating functions, recognizable in all factories, mills, and shops; it treats these and their relationships as the main theme, and the demand and other modifying environmental conditions along with attributes of product and process as sources of variations. After the general procedures of factory operation and control have been developed, or concurrently with that development, applications to typical industries may serve to show the variant forms.

In this type of course, explicit or implicit emphasis is likely to be on genetic similarities underlying the management of all factories, in contrast with the emphasis in the course previously sketched, which tends to dwell upon those inherent attributes or external conditions or pressures necessitating divergences of policy, practice, and organization, and modification of stated principles. Both common basis and necessary divergences and their relationships and mutations afford good case material; but most of the cases appropriate to this second type of course would be on factory arrangement, equipment, departments, organization, and control. The difficulty of pursuing such a course with wholly satisfactory effect emerges as one finds how hard it is for nontechnical students unfamiliar with manufacturing to keep their conceptions of the internal affairs of factories from fog on the one hand, or rule and rote on the other; and the existence of this difficulty becomes the more apparent when the students have to apply their own analytical and constructive thinking to internal factory cases of which their imagined background is more or less incomplete and distorted.

This difficulty in visualizing the manufacturing plant and grasping factory conditions may be taken as one of the arguments for treating the course in industrial management as one in production economics, or on the other hand as an argument equally valid, emphasizing the need for first steps toward an understanding of the elements of factory production in a civilization so largely factory furnished and factory employed. Probably the reasons that make it uncommonly hard to convey an adequate factory background are more or less evident, but two of them may be worth brief note.

Learning to think problems through in so new a mental environment is rather like learning to swim—the strangeness of the medium is more disturbing than the difficulties of the exercise. One cannot well formulate ideas in an unknown idiom, and a good deal of factory thinking is idiomatic. As to supplementary means of clarification, factory visits would help a great deal if suitable factories were near and if time enough for repeated visits were available. Industrial motion pictures fall short of the full three-dimensional effect, but appropriate subjects can be given timely showing at moderate expenditure of time, and the benefit is thought to be substantial.

This awkwardness of thinking in unfamiliar terms is accentuated by the heterogeneousness of the related components that must be thought about and the difficulty of getting a timely grasp of their organic relations and essential unity. These components entering factory operation include such dissimilar subjects as: industrial location, buildings, and manufacturing equipment; design of products, determination and technical control of processes, and technical research; purchasing of materials and parts, and control of purchased, worked, and finished inventories; control of production, giving the word the restricted factory sense; relations with workers of various degrees of skill; administrative and executive organization and control; industrial accounting, and other measurements, comparisons, and reports; and some effort to deal with management in the broader sense of the word. When these apparently unrelated subjects are taken up one at a time the impression gives point to a reported comment of a former business school student that the professor of industrial management gave a lot of interesting courses; the effect is like that of individual orchestra practice. For this reason the case or cases introducing internal factory management ought to be designed to pull the subject together effectively.

Since there is an abundance of suitable case material, and a year gives rather limited time for a management course completely developing either of the approaches that have already been sketched, there will be danger of regrettable abbreviation somewhere in any compromise course directly dividing the time between the two. Therefore, if it be thought wise to combine some study of internal factory control with that of the broader aspects of manufacturing, it may be found advantageous to approach from both viewpoints as many of the cases as lend themselves to it, and a suitable number can be worked out with this twofold approach in mind. No one choice or sequence of material or of treatment is likely to have preponderant general merit; courses properly reflect the varying needs of students and experience of instructors. However, it may be worth while to discuss such a dual approach and the discussion will be less likely to wander if some definite arrangement of case material is taken by way of illustration.

A long first introductory case, dealing perhaps with the survey, purchase, and rehabilitation of a factory, may be used to disclose and sketch three things: first, the relations, interdependence, and organic unity of the several components and functions of a factory; second, the impossibility of estimating a manufacturing prospect or enterprise apart from the physical and economic attributes of its product, and from the demand, the sales contacts, and other environmental determinants; and third, certain generic similarities of all sorts of factories and their problems in control.

A second long introductory case may deal with some such subject as the classification of industrial reports in the office of an industrial engineer, or by a Chamber of Commerce, so as to develop a brief synopsis of various useful bases of classifying manufacturing industries by reference to their attributes or variables both inside and outside the factory itself. Diversities inherent in product, process, and state of the art may be distinguished from those imposed by external conditions and pressures, and the mutual reactions of the two groups can be brought out. The case would serve the purpose of giving an early start to the habit of mentally analyzing and characterizing manufacturing industries.

It might be required that both generic similarities and specific differences should habitually be recognized in subsequent cases, the former helping to correlate experience and develop perception of basic structure, and the latter helping to indicate groupings that aid in carrying over relevant experience and distinguishing that which is probably irrelevant, and in promoting quantitative approach.

A third and last introductory case might discuss basic types and varying aspects of administrative and executive manufacturing organization. For example, an interesting case was that of a large company under several successive conditions: before the war, making the same standardized line that had long been made; during the war, making munitions; and from the end of the war to a recent date, making in enlarged quarters an expanded line, partly old and partly new, with an organization and personnel gradually becoming habituated to this line. Some important general principles of factory and industrial management can be developed from such a case and used in subsequent connections.

After these introductory cases a sequence of case groups may follow, intended primarily to build up a picture of factory operations from within, but without losing clear appreciation of the determining importance of external factors. The groups center on factory functions and divisions; one suitable order of presentation is: physical plant, location, traffic; design, process, standards, quality; purchasing, inventories, storeskeeping; production control closely related with technical control and with industrial accounting; personnel control, including some of its broader aspects; improvement and progress, comprising technical research, current evolution of productive automatisms, and training and development of personnel.

Cases can be drawn from a wide variety of industries so as to afford bases for running commentaries on the effects of both inherent and external sources of diversity. Some examples of inherent sources of diversity that may arise as between industries selected for the several cases are as follows: product characteristics and line; manufacturing processes; relative importance of material, labor, and overhead; degree of technical stability of the art; minimum size of practicable manufacturing unit; degree of dependence on workers' skill and goodwill. External sources of diversity are exemplified in the first course-sketch given in this chapter.

The next division may take up a few comparatively long studies of industries, introduced through cases and supplemented by suitable background material, and may discuss the manufacturing status, problems, and prospects of these industries with only preliminary identification of the character of their factories. This section marked by a viewpoint external to the factory could be expanded at will at the expense of that marked by internal viewpoint.

One alternative for the final division is to start with one or more cases on manufacturing budget and master planning, and afterward rapidly cover selected cases previously assigned and reconsider their grouped and generalized problems, and the appropriate procedure for working out comprehensive plans for the future. If time serves one or more cases may develop the relations between factories in horizontally or vertically integrated groups.

There is room for difference of opinion as to use of formally assigned reading bearing on the cases, as there is also on the advisability of occasional part-hour lectures; during the period of building up factory background at least, both have seemed to have value.

In using cases there is as much room as in other teaching methods for adapting the work to the class and expressing the individuality of the instructor; indeed the generic character of this means of enlisting interested work would perhaps be conveyed better if we spoke of case methods rather than of the case method. The approach from integrated specific situations, through analysis and reconstruction, to sound generalization is the natural approach to the problems of business and aligns with inherent aptitudes. It is well adapted to organize in shortened time the same sort of real self-education that can be derived from business experience and it affords a firm foundation for any subsequent superstructure. Neither any teaching routine nor business experience itself necessarily conveys the higher reaches of interpretive insight and creative imagination, and no new rules of procedure can repeal the ancient laws of education under which good students have always sought—and returned—the inspiration of good teachers.

CHAPTER X

OBTAINING COORDINATION THROUGH THE CASE METHOD OF INSTRUCTION

by GEORGES F. DORIOT

IT IS necessary for a general executive to be able to speak the manufacturer's language and to grasp his problems and at the same time to recognize the problems of distribution and finance. The head of a business organization is called upon both to direct and to coordinate the policies that his company will follow in each of these fields. Perhaps the most important contribution that a general executive can make is this function of coordination. He must see the business as a whole.

In preparing himself for an executive position of the future, the student begins to grasp the importance of proper coordination through the study of actual business problems. Young men usually leave college to go into business without ever having had much contact either with executives or with actual problems. While a certain amount of knowledge is of course essential, the main endeavor of business teaching should be to train students to think clearly and logically and to help them through the transitional stage between the work of college and that of business.

Men entering business must realize that they should be willing to start as far down the scale as necessary. They must recognize that the greatest thing a school can do for them is not to burden them with facts and figures but to develop in them some conception as to the proper way of stating and analyzing problems. The purpose of studying business cases, in contrast to that of studying legal or medical cases, is not to have a man remember a certain number of accidents but methods suggested by a professor in particular cases. Business cases are but tools which make necessary a certain amount of thinking based on stated premises if one is to arrive at a possible solution.

In teaching business by the case method one does not teach any sure way of making money quickly nor is one concerned particularly about answers to problems. The instructor is interested primarily in helping a man select factors of major importance in a situation and, through clear-headed thinking, forcefulness, and mental honesty, develop those factors up to the point where the conclusion comes naturally. Not only thoughts but also logical sequence in their expression are necessary.

Business is not necessarily a science; it is more of an art, in the pursuit of which scientific knowledge and methods can and should be applied. There is no reason why a painter or an artist should not use the results of science, research, and discovery. Any activity such as business, where the human element is an important factor and where premises are still poorly determined and rapidly changing, cannot be referred to as a science without incurring the danger of misconception by the average mind.

Although it is desirable to study subjects of importance in management, finance, distribution, accounting, and statistics, students should be able to coordinate these different fields and activities. The objective is to prevent the individual from becoming too specialized. Students, in addition to their particular capacity along certain lines, should have the imagination and ability necessary to analyze and grasp the component parts of important administrative problems, to follow scientific methods of reasoning, and to be able to decide where effort should be placed. They must learn how to make and carry out plans.

It is necessary to remember that one can no longer succeed in a business enterprise merely by knowing all the intricate details of that business. An executive at the present time must be able to follow trends and discoveries in other lines. Competition is no longer solely between individual companies within an industry but it is also between industries. It is often more necessary to know about the other man's business than it is to know details about one's own, which can be followed and checked by a less experienced person. A man needs to be a coordinator, having the ability quickly to place his finger on the most sensitive points in a business situation. He is only entitled to be a critic when the realization of the point to be criticized in his mind automatically means a constructive idea. He must realize that there is nothing remaining unchanged, that premises and even scientific facts vary and fluctuate. A business is not to be looked upon now as a tangible undertaking built upon solid and immovable foundations. The purpose is not to reach a point where the business is in perfect equilibrium. The goal is to realize the direction and strength of the fluctuating forces affecting one's business and to adapt oneself to them, as under ordinary circumstances they cannot be modified.

The student should have some idea as to what is meant by general business situations and conditions, and he should develop the ability to sense them, remembering that elaborate business statistics are little more than useful indications. Statistics can be compared with history or experience; they represent the past, never showing a complete and impartial picture of any current situation. It may be well, when listing factors to be considered in arriving at a decision, to study questions set forth by past statistics, but the final and determining factor should never be one based upon a reflection of the past. Experience is very useful, but it is sometimes a hindrance. It is safe to say that in business things very seldom happen twice the same way and that ideas rapidly become obsolete. Thinking too much of, and relying too much upon, experience will inevitably lead to mistakes.

Managing a manufacturing concern does not mean that one's job is to continue to manufacture the product which has been manufactured in the past, in the very buildings and with the same equipment which has always been used. It merely means that manufacturing activities will be selected with a view to making money and showing returns on an investment with which one has been entrusted. It should never be taken for granted that because one's predecessors decided to make a certain type of product in a particular building the following generation should be proud of the fact that the same building is still used and the same product made. One must constantly challenge the usefulness of, and demand for, a product, as well as the particular methods used in manufacturing that product.

Business is always confronted by problems arising from the fact that raw materials are constantly fluctuating in price, quality, and quantity; that new and improved manufacturing equipment is always being

developed; and that the demand for the finished product is constantly shifting.

Both manufacturing and distribution methods are
constantly changing. For a great many years it was
understood that the main problem in industry was to
produce and that whatever was made could be sold.
At the present time, many claim that the opposite is
true, that anything can be made and the main problem is how to sell it. Neither attitude is entirely correct; it is the proper coordination between the two,
the proper realization of the fact that one cannot go
without the other, which may lead one to some
success.

The first and probably the main thought to consider,
therefore, is that of movement and change. A business which over a period of time continues making
and selling the same product by the same methods is
in danger of having a competitor develop a product
which is of higher quality or lower cost.

Another phase of proper coordination concerns the
relationship existing between banking and manufacturing. A banker should no longer be looked upon as an
intermediary to whom one can go for cash when new

equipment or additional raw materials are required. Because of the fact that few businesses are now privately owned, bankers have had to adapt their relationships to a changed situation in industry. No one sentence can describe that new relationship. The size of the manufacturing company and its importance will determine the problems to be met in the raising of capital, the kind of banking firm that can handle the financing, and the type and quality of money available.

One point to be remembered by manufacturers in this connection is that there is a quality to capital just as there is to raw materials or equipment. The manufacturer who is received by a banking firm of high standing and reputation gets many intangible advantages as well as cash. Those intangibles are often worth a great deal more than the money itself, not only to the manufacturer but to the stockholder. For a long time to come the banking firms of highest repute, those that consider themselves not as mere intermediaries for manufacturers and stockholders but that realize their responsibilities as well, will naturally be asked to finance the highest grade of manufacturing companies. Such banking houses realize that at the present time money should not be lent merely because past operations have been successful or because certain arbitrary, and often meaningless, ratios meet expectations.

The present relationship between bankers and manufacturers brings up several dangers to be guarded against. Bankers have an excessive desire to merge or increase the size of manufacturing companies whether or not such actions are justifiable and they seem to believe that the larger a company is the better off it will be. A banker will generally try to gauge the worthiness of a manufacturing company purely on an analysis of the past. Another fallacy, altogether too prevalent in banking circles, is the belief that several weak companies placed together will make a strong one. There have been many cases also where bankers have been unable to see that merging several companies doing well would undoubtedly mean a complete failure for each of the component parts.

Bankers have attempted to specialize in certain industries, so becoming expert and reducing costs of investigation. This attempt is dangerous because it leads the banker to believe himself able not only to advise but to manage. It has one advantage, however, in that small companies may be able to borrow from a fairly large bank, which without specialization would not bother with such a small manufacturing unit. Ordinarily a large bank is unwilling to become interested in a small company, since the investigation is almost as expensive as for a large company and since the amount of time spent by the bank and the responsibility involved are as great, while the sale of securities will net only a small return.

It might be advisable to look at manufacturing problems with these factors uppermost in one's mind: cost, volume, and quality. The natural and desirable tendency at the present time is to decrease costs of production, a step which requires a criticism of the company's present aims and the methods now utilized to accomplish those aims and the formulation of constructive policies with respect to many things such as cost of capital, taxes, reserves, standardization, simplification, methods of wage payment, research, substitution, purchase of equipment, manufacture versus outside purchase of parts, mergers, volume of production, and quality of product.

It must be remembered that a manufacturing unit should, above all things, be flexible, readily adjustable to quantitative or qualitative changes in demand, and that there is no justification for carrying on a manufacturing operation on any product or part of a product unless an adequate return upon the investment is being earned.

No system of any sort will ever take the place of clear thinking and common sense. Business problems should be attacked with complete mental honesty, with a fresh point of view, and without prejudice or predetermined ideas. Otherwise false conclusions are bound to follow. The most effective method of instruction, therefore, is the type that forces the student to think for himself and to coordinate those thoughts in terms of actual business problems.

CHAPTER XI

THE CASE METHOD OF TEACHING ECONOMICS

by HOMER B. VANDERBLUE AND CHARLES I. GRAGG

WHILE the discussion which follows places the main emphasis upon the case method as a means of teaching economics to students whose objective is the practice of business, it is believed that many of the conclusions set forth will apply also to the study of economics by other students, whether they plan to participate in government service, to become teachers of the social sciences, or to enter other learned professions.

Adam Smith had a profound influence not only on English government but also on the business men of his and later days. The effects of his writings were felt in foreign lands as well as in England. Manufacturers, tradesmen, and bankers lent attentive ears to the fundamental doctrines which he announced, mainly because he voiced the argument for free trade and the widening of markets. In the days immediately preceding and following the publication of his volume the Industrial Revolution was creating a surplus of products that must find a market outside England.

During the century and a half which has elapsed since the appearance of the *Wealth of Nations,* the formal statement of economic principles has largely continued in the tradition of the classical economists; business men, however, have found other economic problems than those of free trade to be of governing importance. The art of business has progressed rapidly, but no true science of business has yet evolved. Not unnaturally, the question often has arisen whether economics might not contribute largely to the development of such a science. Use of cases setting forth the problems of actual business life as an aid in the teaching of economics (especially as the problems are all real) promises to serve as an aid in bridging the gap between academic reasoning and business practice. If "teaching" be taken to embrace not only classroom instruction, but also analysis and elaboration of the doctrines to be put forth, case instruction in economics may well contribute to the translation of economic theory into business science.

It is not the purpose of this chapter to reiterate what is said elsewhere in this book as to the broad philosophy of the case system. We have chosen to discuss that system simply with reference to the peculiar circumstances which affect the teaching of economics. These circumstances grow chiefly out of the fact that there is extant a large body of well-developed doctrine dealing with the principles of economics. Each division of the subject has been submitted to thorough analysis and exposition; the history of economic theory is in itself a substantial study.

This is in direct contrast with the situation in many strictly business subjects. Until the last quarter century, almost nothing had been published of the inner workings of the business enterprise as they relate to the actual conduct of affairs. Business literature was pretty poor stuff, by and large. The task of learning and interpreting the facts of business policy and conduct has received nothing like the attention which for so long has been bestowed on the study of economic theories. The teacher of business has been handicapped, therefore, but, on the other hand, he has had a relatively free hand in choosing the method as well as the material for his teaching. There is no body of approved doctrine, controversial or otherwise, which the business teacher is asked to impart to his students. Business situations vary so greatly that simple generalization is difficult. The teacher of economics, on the other hand, is typically expected to draw largely, or perhaps wholly, upon the accumulated and current philosophy of his science. He can scarcely do other than select his teaching methods with that expectation in mind.

Cases may be used either as an adjunct of a formal course, to give concrete illustration to the theories, or as a basis of a course in business policy which emphasizes the practical incidence of economic principles on business problems. Thus they may be used to present the essential facts concerning a variety of economic situations in order to give a setting of reality to the study of formal economic principles. The sequence of the cases may be planned deliberately to follow closely the outlines widely used by writers on "principles," such as developed by Professor Taussig. They may also be used, however, not primarily as an adjunct to formal teaching of economic principles, but rather as a means of instruction in the incidence of those principles on actual business problems. The purpose here is to develop in students of business practice the ability to recognize the simultaneous workings of several economic theories in given business situations, and consequently to develop well-balanced policies for the effective conduct of business enterprise.

How far, then, and in what ways can cases properly be used in teaching courses of the above-mentioned types? Let us first consider the two chief ways in which cases are used in teaching economics. One way is to use the case as an illustration of a principle which is already available to the student, either in a text or through statement by the teacher. This use of the case is to show the student, in terms of events which he can understand readily, the specific meaning of the principle under discussion. The attempt is not to have the student evolve a business judgment from the case material, but rather to illustrate a conclusion of economic theory already known to him. The case is offered to provide reality and body for the principle; the case serves to make clear the meaning of the principle.

This technique is not new to economic teaching, though its importance has sometimes been overlooked. Thus Adam Smith, in his opening chapter of the *Wealth of Nations,* proceeds to set out the principles of the division of labor and, to make sure that his reader would have no doubts as to how these principles operate, he almost at once sets forth a "case," in which the output of a pin factory is shown to be multiplied many times through the division of labor. But this case is used as an illustration; Adam Smith takes pains to state the exact nature of the principles at work, and to draw conclusions of general significance. The reader is then left with no doubt either as to the facts or as to their significance. Smith did not expect the reader to generalize from the case to the conclusions, but to accept the writer's conclusions the more readily because of the clarity of the illustration provided.

Again, take John Stuart Mill's use of the illustrative case in Book III, Chapter 2, of his *Principles.* This chapter deals with demand and supply in their relation to value, and after concluding that " . . . the utility of a thing in the estimation of the purchaser is the extreme limit of its exchange value. . . . " Mill follows at once with the statement that "This topic is happily illustrated by Mr. De Quincey"; the kernel of the latter's explanation is the statement of several assumed cases, from each of which he draws a lesson. In these cases, of the shopper, of the voyager on a Lake Superior steamboat, the author has presented his conclusions; the cases are the examples which drive home the meaning of the conclusions.

Almost every writer on economic theory makes similar use of illustrative case materials in connection with his text. These cases usually are either suppositional or are real situations greatly simplified in order to bring out clearly the point to be illustrated. They tend to be of the familiar Robinson Crusoe type, rather than to present in complete form the facts as encountered in everyday life.

Sharply in contrast with the illustrative use of cases is the method of presenting cases *without* a simultaneous statement of the principles inherent in the facts of the cases. This method requires that the student himself analyze the case facts and indicate the conclusions of general significance. The student is not told in advance what the case exemplifies, but rather is told to decide for himself what inferences should be drawn from the given data.

That cases can and should be used for illustration in text-writing may be granted without question, but to use them for illustration only can scarcely be termed dependence on the case system. It should be observed here that even for the purpose of illustration the case based on specific facts taken from actual situations has, because of the vividness resulting from its tone of reality, an advantage over the type of case that is fabricated from general knowledge. For the second way in which cases can be used, the student must not be allowed to find the "answer" immediately available but must be led by discussion to work out a tenable opinion of his own. The student must understand the facts of the case and then perform for himself the task of inducing from them one or more principles. His textbook provides the guide, but it does not tell the whole story.

When readings in texts on economics are required in conjunction with the use of independent cases, then the discussion of the cases can be made to reveal not only the student's grasp of the reading assigned, but also his ability to apply it to the sets of facts in the cases. The advantages of the case method in such a procedure are manifold but may be summarized as follows. The student's interest is attracted through the presentation of related facts having the ring of reality; he gains the valuable experience of analyzing those facts for their bearing on the issue in the case. In comparing his judgment with the conclusions of the author or authors to whom reference is made, he must necessarily familiarize himself with the opinions of the author. Knowledge of an independent, outside set of facts serves to stimulate disagreement with existing doctrine and thus furnishes a basis for original thinking.

Previous to the publication of case books in economics, teachers seeking to give reality to class discussion were limited, in general, to making verbal statements of "interesting examples" during the class period. This method, of course, gave students no opportunity to study the facts in advance and gave the teacher no means of presenting sufficient data on any one situation to serve as the basis for effective induction of conclusions. The case method proper meets both these difficulties; it provides students with factual materials for analysis in advance of class meetings; and it permits the setting forth of materials in enough detail to assure realism.

With advanced classes in economics, the advantages of the case method are intensified. If the cases assigned have been selected because they were typical rather than unique, if the facts are given in sufficient detail, the student as well as the teacher has before him the data for drawing his own inferences as a means of testing, qualifying, or perhaps rejecting the conclusions of writers on the subject under discussion. Even more than in introductory courses memory is subordinated to original thinking; the student learns to use the method of induction in facing new problems and is encouraged to develop his powers of creative analysis.

It has been mentioned that a wide chasm has opened between the reasonings of the economist and the workings of the business man. The latter, the "man in the street," finds difficulty in applying to current problems the findings of the economist. The economist, for his part, tends to disregard the day-to-day business problems of industry, choosing rather to devote his attention to matters of broad interest and long-run effects. There is reason to hope that the bridging over of this gap is not too far off; indeed, steps already are being taken here and there to bring the problems of the business enterprise to the knowledge of economists and to reduce the findings of the latter to terms capable of application to current business requirements.

The use of cases can also be of major importance in the development of a course in business economics, a subject which for purposes of the present discussion may be defined as the study of economic principles in their application to the profitable conduct of business enterprise. Neither the study nor the teaching of this subject is in any sense a simple one; its difficulties equal the difficulties of making correct decisions in the conduct of a business. Economic reasoning usually is predominantly of the deductive type; it makes assumptions and then, isolating one problem after another, comes to deductions as to what will happen when one factor changes, by making the hypothesis that "other things remain equal."

However logical the conclusions reached by this method, the business man cannot apply them without qualification, for in business nothing remains the same; the effects of one policy cannot safely be isolated from other policies. The business man, or the student preparing himself for the conduct of business, must learn to apply economic laws to his own problems effectively, if he is to use those principles at all. In his application he must face the requirement of coordinating the several principles at work in a given situation; he must first recognize and isolate the principles, and then reach a balanced judgment as to what course of action will yield the most satisfactory results.

It is in teaching business economics as a means of helping prepare students for business management that the use of cases can serve to carry over the teachings of economic theory to the field of actual endeavor. Suppose, for instance, that the subject of *profits* is being taken up in a course on business economics. If cases are not included in the program, the procedure might be to assign various readings which would present various phases of the subject. Are profits merely the wages of management, or are they the residue after all wages, as well as the other usual elements of expense, have been deducted from revenue? The type of lecture or class discussion which takes place under these circumstances can be visualized readily. The aim will be to establish the point of view which seems the more tenable, after all the implications and ramifications of the question have been considered. Yet the student may have little or no realization of what the conclusion means in any specific situation; possibly he would remain unfamiliar with the way in which the question would arise in business operations.

Now the same subject can be approached by the use of a case or a series of cases, and the student can be led to appraise the contrasting doctrinal viewpoints through trying to find a tenable solution for the specific case at issue. Let us assume that we have a case describing briefly the operations of a business enterprise such as a manufacturing corporation. The corporation's earnings statements show that for several years net losses have been reported. Income has not even equalled the interest charges that might have been made on capital invested. But among the expenses may be large sums paid to executives, as well as the other customary charges such as rental, wages, taxes, and so on.

The class discussion proceeds to consider whether part of the salaries of executives should not be regarded as profit, and, in any event, whether the corporation's existence is economically justified in view of its earnings record. Without following out in detail the course of the discussion, we may conclude that the case approach to the subject promises to leave the student with at least as full a grasp of the philosophy of the subject as could be given him without the case discussion. Furthermore, it provides him with what he could not readily secure otherwise, an understanding of the controlling importance of the subject for the conduct of a business, as well as ability to recognize the existence of conditions which make urgent the question of determining and justifying the amount of profits. To accomplish these objectives, both the presentation of typical, realistic cases, and the requirement that students do original thinking in reaching well-balanced conclusions suitable to the specific facts, are needed.

But attainment of these objectives is not the only advantage of the case system. The outlook of the teacher himself can be broadened, on the one hand,

and, on the other, narrowed to a point of increased effectiveness by the very process of preparing and studying cases for instruction purposes. If the teacher is directly concerned with the securing of the original case materials from business firms, his opportunities for learning first-hand facts are obviously many. And in any event the inductive analysis needed in preparing to discuss each case must serve to stimulate new thinking on old problems, and the recognition of implications which otherwise might go wholly unperceived. Economics as a science can hardly fail to benefit from these collateral advantages accruing to the teacher through the use of cases.

CHAPTER XII

THE CASE METHOD IN TEACHING GRADUATES AND UNDERGRADUATES

by Cecil E. Fraser

BECAUSE the case method of teaching business was first developed to its greatest extent in a graduate school, there has grown up a natural feeling on the part of many of our ablest teachers that this method of instruction is unsuited for undergraduate classes. This impression is most unfortunate. While a milder form of treatment is perhaps necessary in introducing younger men to a subject than would be the case with more mature students, it is the application of the method rather than the method itself that occasionally requires modification.

From a small beginning in the teaching of graduate students, the use of law cases and medical cases has grown until now a large majority of the undergraduate courses in these subjects are reported to be taught by the case method. While the study of business is still too young to have progressed far along this road, it is safe to say that in this field as well there are perhaps a greater number of undergraduates than graduates who are taught on this basis.

The professor in an undergraduate department who is a pioneer in introducing an improved pedagogical system often has a serious problem before him. In many schools he is an overworked individual teaching from three to five separate subjects and having no stenographic or clerical assistance to relieve him of the burden of endless detail. Not infrequently he is a member of numerous committees which are sometimes important but which in the aggregate seem to consume an inordinate amount of time. Under such conditions he is indeed fortunate if by working overtime he can complete the academic detail that has fallen to his lot before the summer vacation. Not infrequently he has barely completed this academic routine when he is either called upon or feels the financial necessity to teach in the summer school.

Under such conditions it is indeed a courageous man who assumes the burden of changing his undergraduate courses from the tried and true lecture method to the use of cases when it is obvious that such a step entails an additional sacrifice on his part. No instructor can ignore the tremendous amount of time that is necessary to prepare himself to conduct a case discussion in which it not infrequently falls to his lot to answer questions rather than to be continually the aggressor in this field. Yet enough undergraduate instructors have assumed this burden with sufficient success to indicate clearly the soundness of the case method of instruction and the very real rewards that fall to the lot of the man who has made this sacrifice.

In those undergraduate courses, however, where an instructor blazes a new trail and attempts to place his course on what he believes to be a better basis, he finds the new path rough and difficult compared with the well-trodden road which he and his predecessors before him have followed with perhaps but slight deviations for a period of years. Under such conditions he often finds that a professor in an adjoining classroom whose well-polished lectures and perennial jokes cause the students no mental effort is frequently more popular and his course more sought after than his own initial and perhaps uncertain attempts.

Many of his students, moreover, are primarily interested in outside activities; the winning of the applause of the crowd on the athletic field or of the approbation of classmates in an election infringe directly upon the amount of time which students can give to the preparation for his course. Even under these conditions, when the teacher can fire the imagination of his students, when he can show them the importance of doing constructive thinking rather than developing a sponge-like memory, he finds that the underclassman is basically the same individual that he is a year or two later when he becomes a graduate student.

In most universities the teacher of graduate students finds himself in a slightly different category from that of the teacher of undergraduates. Not only are his students more mature so that they do not have to be led in a discussion to quite the extent the undergraduate student does but also as a rule the graduate classes are smaller. Sometimes, of course, a popular undergraduate instructor teaching his full quota of classroom hours has the added burden of conducting a group of graduate men into the more advanced aspects of his subject. But even in such instances the closer relationship that exists between a graduate student and his instructor and the fact that often the classes are at least partially conducted on a seminar or discussion basis make it somewhat easier for such a teacher to initiate the case method of instruction. The graduate student has already learned that he himself must perform the tasks that have been agreed upon, while the undergraduate too often holds to his preparatory school days when his teacher performed most of the work and all the student needed was a reasonably retentive memory and a willingness to prepare routine assignments according to rules that had already been laid down.

In theory, the purpose of the undergraduate course is to give the student a background of information and a grounding in basic principles that is necessary in an elementary approach to any subject. In the graduate schools of literature and arts the advanced courses are based upon a knowledge of this preliminary work. In the professional fields of law and business administration, however, this relationship seldom exists. By far the larger proportion of the graduate students in these fields have studied neither business nor law in their undergraduate courses but on the contrary have kept as far away as possible from these subjects in order to develop a broad cultural foundation on which to build their professional studies in graduate schools. It is frequently erroneous, therefore, to assume that a graduate course in a professional school is based upon a previous knowledge of the subject gleaned from college courses. We must not lose sight of the fact, furthermore, that by far the great majority of our young men who are being educated for business will never attend a graduate school. In the last analysis the goal of the teacher in both undergraduate and graduate courses is to give his students the best possible training for business leadership.

The undergraduate teacher who has the best interest of his students at heart (and what worthwhile teacher has not) must realize how short the period is before his students must embark on their chosen careers. Whether these young men must remain for a long period of years in routine positions where their narrow outlook and monotonous experience may actually undermine their ability to develop a broad executive viewpoint later in life or whether they forge ahead to positions of importance within a relatively short period while there is yet time to develop imagination and leadership depends, of course, to some extent upon the caliber of the men themselves and upon the fickleness of chance. There is no denying the fact that a great many successful men have been neither blessed nor cursed with a college education.

Every educator knows in his heart that he cannot supply natural qualities that are lacking in his students. The purpose of the training that he is striving to give is to develop latent qualities in such a way as to broaden the lives of his students and to increase their usefulness to the greatest possible extent in whatever work may fall to their lot. If the case method of instruction has merit over other methods of instruction in reaching these ends, the instructor who lacks the courage or the ambition to lead his undergraduate students as far as possible in this endeavor has a very grave responsibility.

The case enthusiast in either graduate or undergraduate work, however, does well to admit that there are certain phases of teaching that do not lend themselves to this form of instruction so readily as to the lecture and textbook system. Historical developments of our currency and of our banking system, for example, are better presented in exposition than in a discussion of what is now ancient history. Less important phases of industrial development also may be treated from an informative rather than an argumentative standpoint; in an analogous way the business executive is furnished with reports and other information which he brings to bear on the solution of one of his major problems.

Many instructors in both graduate and undergraduate work have come to feel that the training of the mind in the solution of cases is perhaps of even greater importance for the future business man than for the prospective lawyer or doctor. The law is notorious for its relatively slow rate of change in spite of the tremendous number of new bills that are passed at each session of our legislative bodies. While new discoveries are made in the field of medicine almost daily, many of the same forms of disease attack the present generation in much the same manner that they did its grandfathers. Some changes in the fields of law and medicine are of course taking place, but changes in the field of business have been so rapid that it is almost certain that a conclusion reached a few years ago is open to serious question under current conditions. While the importance of underlying principles and the development of a proper perspective from a study of old cases cannot be overemphasized, the fact remains that the determination of the problem and its actual solution are in themselves valuable training for future business leadership.

It must not be concluded, furthermore, that in either graduate or undergraduate courses it is sufficient merely to develop the power of analysis, important as this attribute may be. The successful business leader of the future, like his successful predecessor, must take constructive steps if his business is to move forward. While the analysis of a problem may disclose many weaknesses as well as points of strength, it is not the job of the executive to adopt continually a negative attitude but rather to take steps to combat those weaknesses or to move ahead in spite of the defects if the results and the amount of risk involved warrant such action. It is of paramount importance, therefore, that the teacher of both the graduate and the undergraduate student should go beyond the development of mere analytical ability and should foster zealously the development of a sound, constructive outlook if our business leaders of the future are to meet courageously the social and business obligations that are certain to be placed upon them.

CHAPTER XIII

THE CASE METHOD IN TEACHING BUSINESS EXECUTIVES

by Harry R. Tosdal

When the proposal was made to develop a summer session for business executives, there arose immediately a number of questions, particularly concerning the possibility of the Harvard Business School's satisfying a need which it knew existed for bringing certain types of training to active business executives. Requests had been received from time to time from business men for some arrangement which would permit those who had not had the opportunity of taking a business course to get some training comparable to that which is furnished to members of the regular session. Comments sometimes took the form of complaints or expressions of regret that many younger executives with considerable experience in business could not have the benefit of the training.

After consideration there was little doubt in the minds of the faculty and administration that certain specific needs for extension of the school's work existed. In the first place, the need of business for men of broad understanding at times conflicts with the general policy of many companies that promotion from within is desirable. Men who were in line for promotion to more responsible positions were not eligible for such promotion in some cases because they lacked the broader point of view necessary for higher executive positions. If some method could be devised for stimulating them to get out of a rut or to get them into a broader way of looking at things, it would be more profitable from several points of view to promote such men than to try to work in some other persons who did not have the benefit of detailed experience with the company. In some cases it would undoubtedly be more profitable to try to broaden and enlarge the understanding and scope of an executive's grasp of present and future jobs by training him after he has had a good deal of experience. The recency of collegiate business training makes it extremely likely that in most organizations capable men are to be found who have grown up with the business, but who, owing to the routine of business or to the nonexistence of broad training available at the time they started, lack certain characteristics of understanding necessary for successful promotion.

Furthermore, in an age of specialization such as ours, it is likely that men who are being groomed for general managerial positions are deficient in their understanding of one or more of the branches of the business. With the greater complexity of business it becomes increasingly difficult, time-consuming, and expensive to have a man acquire by experience a thorough grounding in all the various phases of business management. Even were such a process completed, the lack of an external point of view might militate against his success. Again, there are undoubtedly cases in which it is desired to facilitate the transition of men from one field to another. It may be discovered that a man who has abilities peculiarly suitable for one department has been located in another department. From another point of view, a man who has been in a foreign field for a good many years may, for personal or other reasons, come back to the firm's headquarters.

Because he has been out of touch with the domestic field, a brief course of training may facilitate the transition.

The limited experience of the school in its summer sessions has brought out some other interesting reasons for taking the various courses. Smaller independent business men, well embarked upon careers, have found that discussion of common problems with men from various industries and various sizes of firms tends to give them confidence in their approach to their own problems and to enable them to avoid some of the mistakes which larger firms, through ability to call upon better or at least more different types of men, are not so likely to make. It is probable that further experience will show new needs and variations of the few which have been mentioned.

It was less clear that the needs which we believed to exist could be satisfied by courses given as in the regular session. After that it became fairly obvious that the courses which dealt with specific managerial jobs were likely to be the first to attract the attention of executives. Our experience, however, does not warrant the conclusion that courses in certain more general phases of business, which have in later years demonstrated their practical applications, will be neglected. For purposes of experiment, as many types of courses have been tried out as could be satisfactorily arranged.

The more difficult question concerned the teaching method to be used, for the success of the special session would depend upon the effectiveness of the teaching. Some discussion was devoted to the proposition that we would have to start from scratch for the summer school and that the method of approach should be considerably changed as compared with that of the regular session. In the summer session we were to deal with experienced business men; in the regular session we were dealing, for the most part, with men of no or very limited business contact. The general conclusion was that the lecture method possessed no more advantages for the summer session than it did for other work of the school. Except for the very unusual lecturer with unusual material, the stimulation of men to think out business problems was not likely to be the result of the method.

We were compelled to lay down certain essentials to

be met by any method which gave a promise of being satisfactory in the teaching of executives. These might be stated briefly. First, the method must be one which deals with practical materials, with the things that business men will recognize as business. Preferably such material should be presented in a form closely analogous to business practice. Second, the method must cause the student to put enough thought and effort into the course so as to get the mental stimulation and incentive toward independent thinking. Third, it must increase as a whole the power of the student to cope with business problems. Though it must not ignore fact, it must lay more stress upon the way to get facts and the way in which to use them than upon the learning of facts themselves. In short, it must teach business men how to think honestly and directly upon business problems.

Our experience in the summer school and a study of the results led us to believe that the final decision to present the courses in much the same manner as in the regular session, that is, for the most part by the case method, was wise. The requirements were satisfied by the case method, it seemed, more fully than by any other method which might have been used. It is obvious to alumni of the school that the case method deals with practical material, but the use of the case method in teaching executives was strengthened by the fact that in any representative group of business men there was a strong likelihood that similar cases could be cited from the experience of firms represented. When brought out in class discussion the practical nature of the teaching and of the work was soon established. Once the business man felt that the work was practical, he was ready to put his whole effort into it.

Of course, it should be pointed out that the practical nature of the work should not be limited to the cases themselves. Instruction is facilitated if the teacher has knowledge of the actual conduct of business in its details as contrasted with the broad outlines which one gets from printed materials. He must have a sufficient knowledge of the practical steps of business operation so that with this knowledge of actual practice he meets the so-called practical man on a common ground. The case with its detailed factual description is much akin to the type of material which business men look for at meetings and conventions. Business men call such statements of practice and policies and results "brass-tack" material. A concrete case with the necessity for arriving at a decision is business and not merely talk about business. Having gotten a common ground upon which to discuss practical problems, it is not a difficult matter to get the business man interested in carrying reasoning further to the developing of principles which in themselves are usually limited generalizations.

The major work of the executive consists in making decisions upon business problems. The case method presents these problems broadly, in essentially the same manner as they come to the executive. The chief differences lie in details, in nonessentials rather than in the nature of the problems. It is obvious that written problems covering a wide range of industries must usually be more complete than in the form in which they come to the executive for decision, in which background material is usually omitted, but the problems in business vary in completeness of detail, in definiteness, in concreteness just as they do in the case book. In the second place, the case method requires the student to take an active part in the educational process. Problems are assigned for discussion and individuals are called upon for decisions and for discussion of these problems.

Class discussion may seem quite different from any procedure in business, but class discussion can be so directed as to place a class in the group of useful business conferences. The instructor becomes conference chairman, directing discussion in such a way as to secure a decision on problems presented, while decisions must be defended, developing principles, commenting and generalizing upon decisions and principles, always with the purpose of developing power to think. The *ex cathedra* pronouncement is for the most part out of place at this time in case discussions.

It is our experience that business men read the cases and do a great deal of collateral reading and other work suggested to them, and even go further on their own initiative. Men put their time and effort into the study of these situations, try to think out solutions, discuss the cases with one another, with the result that they educate themselves both in class and out of class.

Lastly, as a result of this process whereby men learn

to think in dealing with actual business situations, the case method does develop that power to cope with problems which should be the objective of general training for business executives. Men learn to do by doing; business executives learn to approach their problems by approaching them. No other method gives the opportunity to the business man of taking concrete problems and going through the mental processes which are necessary in practical business operation. As has been pointed out frequently, there is the incidental advantage that mistakes in decisions in problems in the classroom are not so expensive as they might be if made on the job.

CHAPTER XIV

THE COLLECTION OF CASES

by MALCOLM P. McNAIR

To OBTAIN the best results from the use of the case method of teaching business, it is desirable to have a practically continuous supply of fresh case material. This is true for a number of reasons:

1. The factual aspect of business changes with great rapidity. Therefore, even though underlying principles do not change, there arises continually the need for applying them to new problems and issues arising out of new situations. The grocery manufacturer a dozen years ago, for instance, needed to pay but little attention to chain stores in formulating his marketing program. Today, relations with chain stores constitute one of the most important of his distribution problems.

2. Students, for the most part, are not historically

minded; it is easier to interest them in fresh material than in cases that date back several years. The lessons learned in the business depression of 1921 are still important, but cases dealing with the experience of business men at that time are most effective for teaching use if placed in juxtaposition with cases relating to the financial crisis of 1929 and its aftermath.

3. New case material is necessary to keep the instructor mentally alert. He should continually be forced to match his theories and generalizations with new factual situations developing in his particular field. If he reached the conclusion seven or eight years ago that the chain stores were adapted only to the sale of staple merchandise and could not successfully sell style goods, he needs to be confronted with cases drawn from the experience of such chain apparel organizations as Lerner Brothers, the Consolidated Millinery Company, and others.

Also, in the early stages, at least, of the endeavor to teach business by the case method, there is a fourth reason for maintaining a substantial supply of fresh case material, namely, the improvement in the technique of case collection and presentation, which quickly makes obsolete many of the cases more than one or two years old.

In the collection of cases one of the most important lessons to be learned is the necessity for painstaking preparatory work before the actual field work is undertaken. Where case gathering has been most successful, the preparatory procedure has been substantially as follows:

1. The instructor in charge of the particular course has prepared a detailed outline of the points to be covered in his course. This outline, it is important to note, typically is an outline of principles and issues, not an outline of merely descriptive or factual subject matter. Successful course outlines of this type not infrequently have been the result of several years of careful thought and study.

2. This outline has then been translated into notations of particular cases to be obtained. For instance, on a section of a course dealing with types of mergers, notations might appear as follows: "Case on chain grocery company acquiring a meat packing plant"; "Case on department store acquiring another department store in the same city."

3. These notations of particular cases have next been developed into "specifications," of which the following is an instance:

Specification for Case

Issue: Whether variety chain or dry goods chain should operate one or more warehouses or whether it should have goods shipped directly to its stores by vendors.

Background: Describe company as to type, merchandise, number of stores, geographical distribution, and operating results. Describe methods of purchasing merchandise, especially in connection with securing shipments to warehouses or to stores directly. What experience has company had in securing price concessions on advance orders, and to what extent must it bear carrying charges on such orders if made up in advance?

Describe methods of controlling store inventories, orders, reorders, and new merchandise. Explain price policy and method of fixing retail prices: that is, whether by store manager, superintendents, or central office. Give methods of accounting for merchandise, sales, mark-downs, shortages, and returns; and show how the case would bear on these factors. Are vendors willing to give quantity or other discounts on orders which have to be shipped to individual stores? Could deliveries be made more effectively and under better control by company's warehouse, or by vendors? Are some lots of merchandise bought from a number of vendors, or does each vendor supply the entire requirements?

The questions of prompt delivery, adequate store control, merchandise accounting, and control of store operations seem to be the chief ones to be covered in this case. In addition, costs of warehousing and reshipments are important. Find out whether stores have sufficient capacity to care for direct shipments.

Possible Sources: W. T. Grant Company, J. C. Penney Company.

Whether or not the preparatory work has taken the exact form described, it has been found by experience that the collection of cases in any field cannot profitably be undertaken until the instructor in the course has done the essential thinking involved in the steps enumerated.

As regards the personnel and organization for the collection of cases, a variety of plans have been found effective. In some instances, instructors in particular courses have found it desirable to undertake personally a considerable part of the field work. This has been particularly true where an instructor was putting his course on a case basis for the first time. In fact, it is scarcely going too far to say that thorough familiarity with the processes of case collecting and editing is prerequisite to the successful use of cases in the classroom. Any program where instructors in charge of courses undertake to obtain material for a substantial number of cases, of course, implies a teaching staff in the particular department large enough to permit instructors to be away from the classroom for as long periods as two weeks at a time.

Aside from the collection of cases by instructors primarily to gain experience, and except for one or two departments where special circumstances have existed, it has usually been found most effective to use for the task of case collection a special group of field agents without teaching responsibilities. These men, for the most part, have been recent graduates, preferably with some business experience, but also preferably not so long out of school as to have lost touch with the classroom viewpoint. Such men have had to be most carefully selected, for the work of obtaining raw case material requires to a high degree such qualities as persistence, tact, acumen, salesmanship, and ability to size up situations quickly. Not only must a man be skilled as a reporter of significant business facts, but he must be adept in the arts of cross-examination; it is also particularly important for him to know when to take the statements of a business man *cum grano salis*. Then, on top of these qualifications, he must have the ability to organize the raw material into effective cases.

Experience has shown that it is not feasible to divorce the task of collecting the case material from the task of writing the cases. In the latter part of the work, however, the field agent usually must be given some secretarial and editorial assistance. In the last instance, of course, the instructor cannot escape the responsibility for editing and revising the cases into their final form.

Typically, field agents have worked most effectively where they were under the immediate direction and supervision of a particular instructor. This has meant, however, that an instructor with two field agents working for him frequently has had to give as much as half his time to the direction of their work. Consequently in some instances it has been necessary to have a research supervisor intervene between the field men and the instructor. Unless such a supervisor works very closely with the particular instructor, however, this sort of arrangement has many possibilities for the development of friction and inefficiency. It is fair to say that the only really effective type of supervisor is the field agent with two or three years' experience who has decided to stay in academic work and is beginning to fit himself for a junior position on the staff of the particular department.

After a field agent has had some preliminary training, he ordinarily is given a related group of such specifications as that cited on page 145. After discussing these thoroughly with the instructor or research supervisor, a field man telephones or writes for appointments with executives of the companies that have been indicated by the instructor as possible sources or that he himself selects as possibilities. The preliminary interview usually is with one of the chief executives. In this it is frequently necessary for the field man to do a thorough job of "selling" his particular school and business education generally in such a way as to establish confidence and obtain whole-hearted and ungrudging cooperation.

One of the chief obstacles that must be faced at this point is the reluctance of many business executives to divulge what they consider to be confidential information. There are two lines of argument one or both of which are commonly used by the field man to surmount this barrier. The first is to point out to the business executive the desirability of making such information available for general educational purposes. This is a line of argument that is increasingly fruitful of results as time goes on and business executives become more open-minded. The second line of argument is to show the business executive how the identity of his company may be concealed in the statement of the case by changes of name, location, and certain minor circumstances not affecting the particular issue. In this connection an expedient frequently resorted to is the alteration of all quantitative data, such as operating statements, balance sheets, and so on, by multiplication of all figures by some such constant as 1.6 or 0.7.

In the process of securing a chief executive's consent to obtaining case material, it usually is necessary to avoid any suggestion of a *quid pro quo* basis. It is occasionally true that a business man is confronted with a particular problem on which he would like to have the opinion of one or more members of the school's staff, or which he would like to have presented to a class as a problem for a written report with the privilege of examining some of the best student reports. These instances are rare, however; and in general a field agent must base his plea for cooperation on the desirability of contributing to the cause of business education rather than on any immediate benefits to accrue to the particular concern.

After he has convinced the chief executive of the desirability of cooperation, the field agent indicates the particular persons in the organization whom he wishes to interview for the case he is trying to obtain. This, of course, frequently necessitates making an appointment for another day. In working on such a specification as cited on page 145, when the field agent reaches the particular persons who are in a position to give him the facts, he cannot proceed by asking, "Have you any cases on warehousing?" because business men do not think in such terms. He will rather begin by asking what policy the company has adopted with respect to warehousing, whether there have been any recent decisions as to more or less extensive warehousing, what the circumstances were that brought up the question, and so on.

In this way the field agent gets the business man to talk in his own language about the company's policies.

Then it is the agent's job to detect from such a discussion the point where an important decision was made. From there on, he concentrates on obtaining all the facts and reasons leading up to this decision. To do this he frequently must interview more than one executive and perhaps go back to the company for several subsequent conferences. Not infrequently it may be necessary for the field agent in discussion with the business man to develop latent problems and issues not yet fully crystallized in the executive's mind.

In the course of his conferences the field man makes rough notes and obtains copies of memoranda, operating statements, and other pertinent data. Then if he is working locally, he returns to his office at the school and at the earliest convenient time organizes the material into a rough preliminary draft of the case. If the field man is away from the vicinity of the school on a trip, he may obtain material for a number of cases before returning to put them into written form. Usually it is not effective for a field agent to stay out more than two weeks at a time or undertake to obtain material for more than half a dozen cases before he begins the task of writing and organizing.

After the field agent has written the first draft of a case, one copy of this goes to a secretarial assistant for revision in form and expression, and another copy to the instructor. If the work of case collection is to be successful, it is necessary for the instructor immediately to give his attention to the rough drafts of new cases. Particularly, he will examine the case to find out whether there is a clear issue involved and whether this issue fits logically into the outline on which he is working. Next, he examines the case carefully to see whether all the pertinent facts are available on which a decision of the issue was or should be based.

Quite often at this point it is necessary for the instructor or research supervisor to indicate additional information which the field agent needs to obtain before completing the case. After getting any necessary additional information and after obtaining the suggestions of the secretarial assistant, or "case reader," as to form of presentation, the field agent writes the case in final draft, sending one copy to the instructor, one to the general case files, and a third copy to the company for inspection and approval. This does not end the process of editing and revising, however, since before such a case is mimeographed for class use or published in a case book the instructor usually finds it necessary to work it over again with a great deal of care and thought to make it fit smoothly into the particular section of his outline.

No one best formula has been evolved for the presentation of a business case. One fairly common type of case begins with a succinct statement of the type of concern involved and the particular issue faced; follows this with a brief statement of the immediate circumstances leading up to the emergence of the issue; goes on to a description of the general background of the concern, the nature of its products, markets served, channels of distribution, size of company, organization, corporate and financial structure, and the like; presents a fairly detailed statement of pertinent facts and reasons bearing on the particular issue; and ends with a statement of the company's decision or, if a decision has not been reached, with a question as to what that decision should be.

The term "case" is used to denote a case where the decision is stated, while "problem" is used to denote a case which ends with a question rather than a statement of the company's decision. Although the tendency at the outset was to use "problems" almost exclusively for teaching purposes, experience indicates that for most pedagogical purposes "cases" are equally useful.

Whatever the precise form taken by a case, there is always present for the field agent and the instructor the question as to how high a degree of selectivity should be employed in presenting the facts. From a strictly realistic standpoint, several different issues may be interwoven in a given business situation; and even if there is only one issue, the facts relating to that issue are almost sure to be intertwined with other facts that are not pertinent. It is part of the business man's task in his thinking to single out issues and narrow down the facts to those that are strictly relevant. While it is good training for the student, particularly the advanced student, to go through a similar process, the pedagogical consideration is nearly always present that students can better learn to think for themselves in a given situation if their attention is confined to a particular issue and the facts relating to that issue. Thus the field agent and the instructor between them usually find it necessary to bring the facts in a case into a somewhat sharper focus than exists in the actual situation. In almost any course, however, it is advisable to have a few cases, for "diagnostic" purposes, which approach photographic realism in their reproduction of factual situations. Usually it is not found desirable, however, to introduce artificially any irrelevant material for the purpose of throwing the student off the scent.

Since descriptive statements of general background may occupy a good deal of space and consequently take a considerable part of the student's time for reading, it is frequently possible to develop a series of three or four or half a dozen cases, each with a different issue but all based on the same company and consequently employing but a single statement of background. It is to be noted, however, that the use of separate cases in a situation of this kind is preferable to the use of a single omnibus type of case with a number of different issues.

It has been found from experience that a vast majority of cases must be collected at first hand from individual companies. It is practically never possible to obtain satisfactory cases at second hand from some individual, no matter how fully conversant he may be with all the facts in a particular company or industry. Although some use can be made of published data, in general this source of case material is distinctly secondary in importance. Occasionally a financial prospectus issued in connection with the sale of securities may contain enough facts to constitute a case. From time to time, also, law cases, particularly those involving such business problems as price maintenance or trademark rights, may be used as business cases. But ordinarily it is necessary to go behind such statements and obtain additional facts at first hand from the companies concerned. On rare occasions it may be possible for an instructor who is thoroughly familiar with factual situations of a given type existing in a number of companies to write so-called "arm-chair," or fictitious, cases, or more properly "examples." The use of such examples for teaching purposes is largely confined to the illustration of accounting and statistical principles or other cognate situations where the underlying principles are mathematical in character. Even in these instances, however, it is distinctly difficult to invest such cases with an aura of authenticity.

In length, cases may range from one to thirty pages or more. The average of the cases obtained usually lies somewhere between four and six printed pages. Of this type of case, under the best conditions, a competent field man cannot turn out more than one and one-half to two a week, and the average output is not much above one a week. This means that the average cost of case collection, including salaries, travelling expense, secretarial and stenographic assistance, and supervisory overhead, is unlikely to be below $100 per case.

CHAPTER XV

THE PREPARATION FOR TOMORROW'S PROBLEMS

by PHILIP CABOT

THE teaching methods of business schools in the United States are beginning to divide into two systems which are radically different in both theory and practice. For convenience they may be earmarked as the method of precept, or the lecture system, and the method of experience, or the case system, and we can hardly evade questioning which is better adapted to the conditions of our time.

The method of precept is as old as history. Hallowed by tradition and stamped with the approval of all great teachers and prophets, it needs no explanation and no defense, for it can stand upon its record. But it should be noted that it was designed for use, and has been mainly used in practice, under conditions where life was practically static, and where all that was necessary, or even possible, was to instruct the young in the ancient wisdom of their fathers, fill them with love and respect for the achievements of the past, and teach them to read the lessons of history. The ancestor worship of the East, which has developed in China the finest system of personal conduct of which we have any knowledge, is a good example of what this method can accomplish. But it was designed to deal with a static condition and tends powerfully to maintain that condition; where conditions are in a state of constant and rapid change it may produce unexpected results.

The method of precept was the child of the patriarchal system in which discipline and conformity were the cement which bound the members of the tribe together and enabled them to survive in the struggle with their neighbors. These were the highest, if not the only, virtues for the common man and were enforced with all the military and religious authority that kings and priests could bring to bear. The educational system of the Church and the legal system of the State were evolved for this purpose and they were so successful that, as we now see, the capacity to vary or evolve has been stamped out of most races upon the earth, and their culture and civilization after rising to a certain level have become static. For such peoples and such conditions the method of teaching by precept is ideal. All that a young man needs for success in life is to know the wisdom of his fathers.

But those who live in the United States face a wholly different situation. Not rest but change is the basic condition of our lives, and even change is seen to move from year to year at an accelerating pace. This observation applies, of course, only to the material circumstances of our daily lives and especially to the economic or business world. The laws of the Cosmos, including all the moral and spiritual relations of men to each other and to their Maker are, so far as we know, immutable. But the environment of our daily lives is changing with bewildering speed, and it is impossible, therefore, to teach the technique of dealing with that environment which we call business by the ancient method of precept. To instruct a young man today in the best methods of doing business known to his father is merely to mislead him; and even to teach him the best standard practice of today is little better, for it will be useless tomorrow. The principal thing that he must now learn is how to deal with a condition of constant change, and for this the ancient method of precept is ill designed.

In order to employ the method of precept, or the lecture system, the business world must be reduced to a static, or stationary, condition in which the phenomena of business can be confined and described. But in the process the phenomena themselves lose their perspective and even their shape and become mere caricatures of what is really going on.

One way of escape from this dilemma is to substitute for the method of precept the method of experience, to abandon the attempt to teach business technique and to teach instead a method of analysis, or diagnosis, of each new situation as it confronts the executive. This method is known as the case system, which at its best is the nearest practicable imitation of real life. It does not aim to give the student ready-made answers to the problems which it is assumed his business life will present to him. Such an enterprise would be futile, for the questions which he will have to answer have not yet been asked. The question that has not been asked cannot be answered. The problem presented to a business school closely resembles the problem of a medical school. Time was when medicine was taught by textbooks and lectures but the method has been superseded by the clinical method of case teaching where the student has to discover from an examination of the patient what, if anything, ails him. As disease has no existence outside the body of the patient, each case is in some degree unique, and the technique of medical diagnosis is thus evolved.

The problems of modern business are of essentially the same character. No two of them are the same but if the problem can be clearly stated—that is, if a diagnosis can be made—a long step has been taken toward its solution. Without the use of cases the teacher of business today is as helpless as the teacher of medicine.

And there is another important use to which these cases may be put. All cases, if properly reported, illustrate the importance of the time element in business decisions. Today time is of the essence in every such decision and in this respect no two cases are the same. In some business situations, where fashions are involved, the change is very rapid and an accurate judgment of the tempo may be the controlling factor, while in others, like the public utilities, the time factor may be so slow as to be almost negligible. A sound decision on the time element has now become the basis of foresight, for foresight cannot be exercised until what might be called the "time frame" of the problem has been determined. Unless this time element is dealt with skillfully the decision is nothing more than a guess and the business man has fallen to the level of the quack doctor.

But in most of the treatises on economic theory by which business is supposed to be guided the time variable has either been arbitrarily stabilized or ignored. In the past this may not have been a serious weakness but now it is fatal and economic theory will be of small service to business men until this defect has been remedied.

One way of doing this is by a patient study of the actual problems presented by the business world of today. The problems of yesterday are already out of date. Like the medical student and the doctor we want live patients, not dead ones; in fact, the dead ones only serve to verify a diagnosis which was previously made on a live one.

The conclusion would seem to be that business problems skillfully selected and thoroughly reported are the material from which both business students and economic theorists must learn.

33830